Endorsements

Embody Your Inner Goddess is a wonderful and practical journey to help anyone step into the path of divine feminine healing. I highly recommend it for anyone who is ready to apply embodied spiritual wisdom into their life!
– Sahara Rose, best-selling author of *Discover Your Dharma* and host of *Highest Self* Podcast

Embody Your Inner Goddess is a powerful guidebook for anyone seeking radical transformation and self-love. Lauren combines practical spiritual wisdom with vulnerable personal tales in order to create the perfect structure to nurture your personal growth.
– Dr. Neeta Bhushan Nawalkha, best-selling author of *Emotional GRIT* and *That Sucked. Now What?* and host of *The Brave Table* Podcast

Embody Your Inner Goddess is the ultimate guide for those looking to connect and awake their sacred feminine energy within. The book's 7-week journey is based on the chakra system and offers opportunity for reflection and embodiment through writing, movement, breathing exercises, and more – making it suitable as a cover-to-cover practice or a resource for time to come!
– Dr. Sarah Kucera, DC, CAP, author of *The Ayurvedic Self-Care Handbook* and *The Seven Ways of Ayurveda*

In *Embody Your Inner Goddess*, Lauren Leduc lovingly guides us through a journey of soul reconnection and empowerment. Through immersive reflection practices, relatable life lessons and a compassionate voice, Leduc helps us remember the inner spark of our own divinity and encourages us to live with that spark ignited.
– Rachael Cohen, author of *Everyday Plant Magic* and *Infinite Succulent*

Oh this life and the people we get to meet and love on our path! I have been so blessed to be a witness to Lauren Leduc's Journey to Radical Wholeness. Over the last ten years it has been such a joy to watch her embrace, with wild abandon, her fun, playful and sensual nature, to be in her presence as she claims, outright and with conviction, her bright and brilliant light of love and service, and to feel the warmth of her smile! My heart has known, for some time, her sweet smile – and today – I saw that smile as I have never seen it before – with such big laughter as she dances and sways and opens her arms wide to all of life that is just bursting around her. I can't help but want to join in on this wild and fantastic goddess adventure! I want to dance this dance to Radical Wholeness!
– Jennilee Toner, author of *The Perfect Chaturanga: A Comprehensive Guide to the Human Body Through the Practice of Vinyasa Yoga*

Embody Your Inner Goddess

A Guided Journey to Radical Wholeness

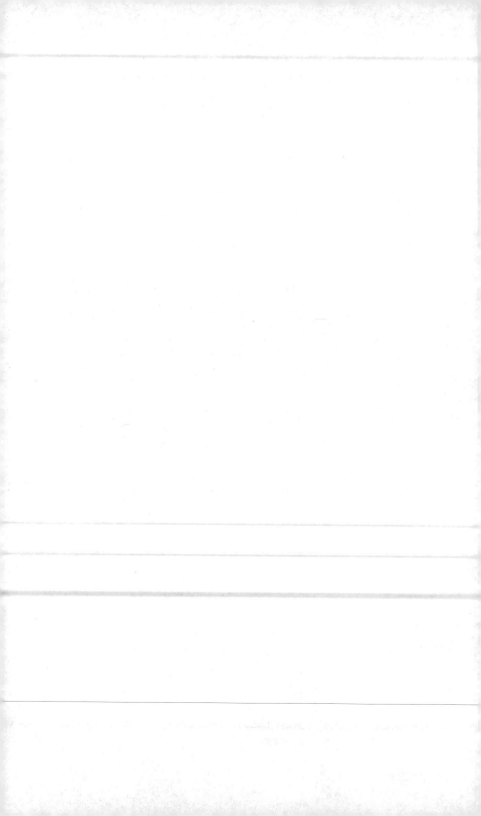

Embody Your Inner Goddess

A Guided Journey to Radical Wholeness

Lauren Leduc

BOOKS

Winchester, UK
Washington, USA

JOHN HUNT PUBLISHING

First published by O-Books, 2023
O-Books is an imprint of John Hunt Publishing Ltd., 3 East St., Alresford,
Hampshire SO24 9EE, UK
office@jhpbooks.com
www.johnhuntpublishing.com
www.o-books.com

For distributor details and how to order please visit the 'Ordering' section on our website.

ISBN: 978 1 80341 362 4
978 1 80341 363 1 (ebook)
Library of Congress Control Number: 2022945264

A CIP catalogue record for this book is available from the British Library.

Design: Lapiz Digital Services

UK: Printed and bound by CPI Group (UK) Ltd, Croydon, CR0 4YY
Printed in North America by CPI GPS partners

Contents

Dedication

To my baby, Gemma. I bow to the Goddess in you. I pray every day that I'll be the mama that you need. Thank you for choosing me.

Acknowledgments

First, I thank my lactation consultant, Summer Friedmann, for kickstarting my breastfeeding journey with Gemma. Without your help in establishing a nursing relationship, I surely couldn't have written this book, as most of it was written on my phone with baby at my breast.

I must acknowledge my partner and husband, Arthur, for your endless support and encouragement. I am so proud of our journey together, and am so grateful for our shared life and family. It's really beyond my wildest dreams.

I am incredibly grateful for every person mentioned in this book, especially my parents who just celebrated 42 years of marriage. To anyone mentioned in this text, I love you deeply.

I bow to my teachers, especially Jennifer Yarro, Jennilee Toner, Vidya Heisel, Sahara Rose, and Neeta Bhushan. Thank you for passing such life-changing wisdom to me.

Thank you, Rashida, for lending an ear during this process, asking so many wonderful questions, and being an overall great friend.

I thank my yoga community in Kansas City. Thank you for providing me space to hone my skills and grow as a teacher.

Thank you to all the witches and wild women who came before me. Your sacrifice is my gift.

I send my greatest gratitude to every culture and lineage who developed and inspired many of the practices and wisdom in this book, especially to those who have stewarded the practice of yoga for millennia.

Om Shanti, Om Peace.

Introduction

My Story

Goddess, I am truly honored to guide you on this 7-week journey and for us to ascend and connect in our wholeness together. Thank you for trusting me and this co-creation with Spirit to help you live your highest expression, connect with your purpose, and usher in the rise of the sacred feminine.

I share bits and pieces of my own story throughout this book, not because it's particularly remarkable, but because it's human. Growing up as a sensitive person, I never felt whole. While I was a bright and joyful child, many outside influences affected my internal landscape, eventually making me believe the lie that I am not enough. I carried familial and ancestral trauma, felt bombarded with messages from culture and media, and unfit for a linear and patriarchal world. While I carried the privilege of a cis white body, I still never felt I fit in or was made for this life.

This not-enoughness and discomfort in my own embodiment led to many years of disfunction including eating disorders, depression, anxiety and debt. I tried to fill the perceived hole inside of me with substances, romantic involvements, and denial.

Eventually, I knew I had to make a change. There was always something inside me that knew I was made for MORE than this. I began my healing journey, and after many years of self-inquiry, spiritual work, and support from loved ones and teachers, I now live a life I love. I'm a mother, a wife, business owner, a yoga teacher, and a Spiritual Life Coach. Most importantly, I know who I TRULY am, divine incarnate, just like YOU. Human, imperfect, and holy.

My experiences and story have been the fertile soil for my life's purpose and I have had the honor of supporting many people on their spiritual path. It is my greatest wish as I share vulnerably with you, that you feel inspired to connect with your own story. As an intuitive, a visionary, and a healer, it is my belief that as we embrace and embody the sacred feminine, we will usher in a new age of peace, collaboration, respect for nature, and connection with Spirit. Together, as we embody our Inner Goddesses and live radically whole lives, our interwoven vibration will reverberate into the world. By loving ourselves, by healing ourselves, we create heaven on Earth. Are you ready?

Who This Book Is For

This book is for anyone who ever feels like they are too little or too much. For anyone who ever feels stagnant and stuck. For anyone who ever feels like there is more out there for them. Who feels like there is so much more inside of them waiting to be revealed. For anyone lost. For anyone lonely. For anyone caged. For anyone who has ever felt broken. This book is also for anyone already treading the spiritual path, who has had glimpses of their truest selves, but who needs inspiration, support, and structure.

This is as much for me as it is for you. If there is even a seed of hope within you, this is your invitation to nurture this seed and watch it grow into a garden beyond your wildest dreams.

Most importantly, this book is for anyone wanting to connect more deeply with their authenticity, weirdness, joy, spirituality, and femininity. No matter your gender, you can benefit from this book, especially if you have ever felt marginalized in this society. Female, femme, trans, or gender non-conforming, this journey is open to you. As a note, since I am speaking directly to your sacred feminine side, I use the pronouns she/her as well as Sister, Queen, and Goddess to refer to you on this journey. However, I recognize and honor that gender and gender expression are personal and unique to each reader. The human experience isn't black or white, but in the grey, and as we usher in more balance of spiritual polarities of masculine and feminine, we also invite in integration and celebration of the wild, mysterious, and indefinable divine.

More on Feminine and Masculine

When I describe feminine and masculine in terms of Source or the divine, I'm not speaking of sex or gender, rather polarities that exist within everyone and everything. Feminine refers to lunar, cool, passive, cyclical, and receptive energy. Masculine refers to solar, hot, linear, and penetrating energy. We all hold both within us, at varying levels of balance or imbalance. In a yogic practice, we are striving to balance our energies and integrate our inner polarities.

Historically, for many thousands of years, human culture has been patriarchal, where men and masculine energy hold power and women, trans, and queer people have been largely excluded. This imbalance translates to a global society of war, competition, and domination. Furthermore, while many cultures around the world originally worshipped the Goddess, as patriarchy spread and dominated, organized religions have actively and systematically suppressed the sacred feminine, especially in Western cultures. This leaves feminine-identifying people not only without political and familial influence and power, but removed from their own divine identity. Due to this imbalance, the whole world suffers.

So while we all hold the polarities of feminine and masculine, for many people, the masculine dominates and the feminine cries to be noticed, embraced, and emboldened. Each of us individually is a microcosm of the macrocosm, meaning, a small and complete representation of the whole. This journey to embody your Inner Goddess is so incredibly important not only to bring more balance to your own being but to the Earth. We are all connected and when you do the work of ushering in the sacred feminine, we all benefit.

Your Inner Goddess

Your Inner Goddess is your personified personal connection to the sacred feminine. She is beyond any outside teacher, guru, or deity. In her infinite power, wisdom, and compassion she is YOUR highest self. You are her and she is you. This journey is about remembering her, communing with her, and embodying her.

On Embodiment

Embodiment is taking this information out of the mental and theoretical realms and into your own being. Think of your favorite actor or actress. They are likely not only "pretending" to be a character, but fully **being** the character by expressing their essence through all parts of their being, especially their body. As you move through the readings, reflections, and exercises in this book, I invite you to let them seep into every cell. I invite you to not only contemplate and meditate on the various chakras, affirmations, and concepts, but to bring them into every part of your being, especially your body. I invite you to embrace and not bypass the hard stuff. This will invite in the transformation, growth, and grounded experience that you seek.

On Radical Wholeness

I have a secret to tell you. Although the subtitle of this book is *A Guided Journey to Radical Wholeness*, in reality, you are **already** whole. Like me, you might have bought into the story that you are not enough or that you are too much. You might feel like there is a hole inside of you that cannot be filled no matter how hard you try. You may have searched far and wide outside of yourself to feel complete. You might long for a feeling of union, but with what?

Because the divine is within you, you are connected to everyone and everything. You are holy, not "holey". You might forget over and over, but you can always come back home to yourself. This realization or remembering in a world of people who have forgotten is a bold and radical act. Thank you for taking this journey home with me.

The Chakra System

This guided journey is supported and informed through the Chakra System. As you make your way through each week, you'll be introduced to a new chakra and invited to balance it and embody its essence.

The Chakra System, first introduced in Vedic or ancient Indian texts as early as 1500 BC, is a way of meditating on different aspects of the human and spiritual self. Although there are a number of different chakra systems, discovered in deep meditation through ancient mystics, and described throughout Yogic texts, we will focus on the 7-chakra system, informed and popularized in Western culture by 20th century occultists. This is the most current, well-known, and studied iteration of the chakras and what most modern spiritual seekers have an awareness of. While there are many ways to view the chakras throughout cultures and history, I chose this particular system to provide the structure of this journey because of its cultural pervasiveness and its personal effectiveness in my life as a teacher, intuitive, and energy healer.

Chakras are defined as whirling vortexes of life force energy. Life force energy, or *prana*, flows throughout our being along superhighways called *nadis*. Every intersection of these *nadis* or highways creates a whirling vortex of energy, or *chakra*. While in the West, we tend to think about the body as purely physical, the Chakra System exists in a holistic realm that encompasses the physical, emotional, mental, and spiritual planes.

While there are many chakras in the body, the 7-chakra system focuses on only the chakras that exist within our central channel, governing almost every aspect of human life. The main *nadi*, or energy channel, is called *Shushumna* and runs along the spine. To the right of *Shushumna* is *Pingala*, the masculine energy channel. To the left is *Ida*, the feminine energy channel. Together, they spin and intersect along *Shushumna* to create the 7 major chakras.

At the base of the spine is *Muladhara* or the Root Chakra which governs our basic need for survival. Next, in the pelvis is *Swadhisthana*, the Sacral Chakra, which holds our creativity. The upper abdomen houses *Manipura*, the Solar Plexus, our center for personal power. Then, we ascend to *Anahata*, the Heart Chakra, center of love. Next is *Vishuddha*, the Throat Chakra, at the base of the throat, which holds communication. Then, at the forehead is *Ajna*, the Third Eye Chakra, center of intuition. Finally, at the top of the head lives *Sahasrara*, the Crown Chakra, our connection to the divine.

Each section of this book gives you a deeper glimpse into each chakra and a chance to explore, balance, and heal it through readings, reflections, and practices designed to help you embody your Inner Goddess. As you find balance and alignment through each one, you will feel more whole, more fortified with personal power, and more fully expressed.

If you are skeptical of the chakras, I totally understand. It can be difficult to believe in things we cannot see, and which have not been scientifically proven. I don't personally think that you have to believe in the chakras to benefit from their teachings. However, they are a beautifully organized way to understand the self, from your most animal self to your most spiritual. So in the spirit of exploration and curiosity, I invite you to "try it on" and see if it fits. As you are invited to tap into the energy of each chakra, you might find that they are an incredibly beneficial tool for your growth, just as I have.

How to Use This Book

This book is organized as daily readings, journaling reflections, and embodiment practices with each week exploring a different chakra. This isn't meant to be consumed all at once, but to be savored over time. This is an interactive experience, and the more you put into it, the more you will get out of it. I recommend scheduling 20 minutes of time in your calendar every day, a sacred date with yourself, to explore this work. Although you do not need to purchase any supplies to explore the practices, I do recommend a journal to keep all of your reflections in one place and to document your journey.

If you have any friends or loved ones who would benefit from this book, I highly recommend holding a weekly book club or accountability group so that you can explore and discuss this journey together. I find most people get a lot more out of spiritual work when they have the support of a community.

Another way to use this book, especially after completing the 7-week journey, is to use your intuition to choose a "random" page whenever you are needing inspiration or guidance. You may be surprised to find exactly what you were needing.

You can also find additional resources, support, and embodiment practice instructional videos at laurenleduc.com.

Seeking Support

As you are working through this book, there may be topics that feel personally triggering for you. I recommend taking a break and being gentle with yourself if your nervous system needs time to catch up and integrate. This is a marathon, not a sprint. Also, this book is not a substitute for mental health care. If you are experiencing a crisis or would like additional support, I urge you to please seek out a professional mental health provider in your area. There is no shame in seeking support. I have personally done it many, many times.

Your Divine Initiation

Welcome to the work. I invite you to get comfy, make your favorite tea or light a candle, and read the following section:

Sister, I am here to invite you to show the F up in your own damn life. The time for playing small, for shrinking yourself, for hiding your shadows, and for half-assing your life is over.

If you are reading this, if you are interested in embodying your divinity, if you're hungering for the pure freedom of embracing your most authentic and badass self, then know you have **chosen** to be here on Earth at this time. Your heart, your soul, your specific and unique frequency is here to heal humanity and usher in a beautiful new age and the rise of the sacred feminine.

Our foremothers didn't suffer through suppression, enslavement, and persecution for us to not show the F up. Their hidden magic, suppressed through colonial and patriarchal forces, is entwined in your DNA. Codes just waiting to be awoken. Your ancestral magic is ready and awaiting.

Sister, consider this book an invitation to be fully expressed, fully embodied. Consider this the start of a brave journey of excavation, vulnerability, befriending thyself, and leaving nothing swept under the rug.

Sister, I want you to know that ALL parts of you are beautiful. All parts are meant to rise to the surface to heal and be transmuted into presence, joy, and the frequency of radical peace.

Sister, your spiritual journey isn't to transcend the body, to sit in silent meditation alone in the mountains, to curse the body for its sins. Your journey is to let the Universe dance in every cell of your body. To follow the moon. To cover yourself in earth. To swim joyfully in her waters. To commune with your sisters, to be in holy balance with our brothers and siblings. To bleed, to sweat, to cry, to eat, to fuck, to paint, to sing, to nurture, to scream, to dance. To radically trust yourself and nature. To labor ecstatically and birth creations of the highest vibration into this plane.

Your life is a sacred journey and I invite you to leave no stone on this path untread. I invite you to break past your walls that you have built to protect yourself and let the world see the beauty of your vulnerability. To let it be messy. To let it be ugly. To let it be human. Invite every part of you to the dance of life. Embrace all versions of you, past, present, and future, and bathe in her wisdom.

Sister, for many millennia humanity has been off-kilter. We conquer instead of collaborate. We steal rather than share. We submit our spirit to the authority of corruption. We poison our waters. We fight over who is human and who is not. We buy into dogma that traps us in its promise of safety. We are stuck in cycles of trauma and abuse. Sister, we need the Goddess.

She is here to flow within structure. She is safety in the darkness. She is radical intuition that bears more truth than cold rationalization. She is the undertone of power in gentleness. She is the mother, Parvati, the warrior Durga, the muse Saraswati, and the lascivious abundance of Lakshmi. She is here to hold us, to elevate us, to heal us, to help us descend into our bodies and dance with life.

Sister, you have a direct line to the divine and that is your Inner Goddess. I invite you to greet her, invite her into your body, to awaken your codes, to draw her into your root to connect with Mother Earth. To co-create your fullest expression so that you may live your soul's purpose and raise the vibration of humanity.

Goddess, you chose to be here at this time. To awaken to your highest truth. To heal your lineage, yourself, humanity, and the Earth. Goddess, you are the medicine we all need, and the more YOU that comes forth, the more potent the potion.

And to do so, you must show up for yourself. Show up when you feel low. Show up when you feel high. Show up when it's really fucking hard. Drag yourself if you must to your heart, your house of healing. Show up and let Goddess do the rest. You don't have to be perfect, you just have to truly be you. An Earth angel. Goddess incarnate. Sovereign. Powerful. Beautiful.

But it won't happen if you don't show the F up for yourself. Surrender to the process. Dance with the divine. Goddess, the time is now. Show the F up.

Week One

The Root Chakra

We start this journey at our energetic foundation, the Root Chakra, or ***Muladhara***. Located at the base of the spine and pelvic floor, this chakra governs the roots of our existence, our basic needs, our survival, and our security. As we examine these different aspects of self that bind us to our human existence, we are invited to truly go deep into our roots. To consider if our basic needs are being met. To meditate on the beauty and messiness of the physical plane. And to embrace what it is to be safe and at home within ourselves.

I invite you to take a moment and place your hands on your pubic bone or lap. Take several deep breaths and focus your energy and attention on the Root Chakra. See it spinning, a deep red four-petaled flower. Imagine its roots, growing downward and tethering you to the nurturing energy of Mother Earth. Imagine the flower encompassing your stability, foundation, security, and physicality. See it vital to provide the soil, seed, and roots from which you can safely and gloriously ascend to the heavens and your sacred femininity. You might fill the chakra with its sacred sound, Lam, by chanting it deeply three times. Then release with a breath in through the nose, and out through the mouth.

Keep in mind, as you partake in the daily readings, reflections, and practices, that this is the densest chakra. In other words, this chakra holds a lot of our "stuff", much of which we hold unconsciously. I invite you, as you journey through your relationship to your body, childhood, home, money, and other topics that can be triggering, that you be gentle with yourself. I implore you to take pride in turning over stones, some comfortable and some not, and find deep compassion for yourself. Your story, and your foundation, are beautiful and worthy. And you are such a badass for taking this brave journey to realize your wholeness and embody your Inner Goddess.

Root Chakra (*Muladhara*)
Location: Base of the spine or pelvic floor. It also is associated with the legs and feet.
Energy: Survival, Stability, Physicality, Belonging
Color: Red
Sacred Sound: Lam
Element: Earth
Overactive Chakra Symptoms: Stagnation. Greed. Overindulgence.
Underactive Chakra Symptoms: Fear. Insecurity. Disconnection. Scarcity.
When in Balance: We know our basic needs are being met. We feel appreciation and connection to our bodies,

homes, and Earth. We feel abundant and grateful. We are grounded and flexible. We have a strong foundation and are able to connect to the higher chakras.

Connect to the Root Chakra with:

Food: Nuts, Fats, Root Vegetables, Red Fruit

Scents: Black Pepper, Cedarwood, Sandalwood

Crystals: Smoky Quartz, Garnet, Red Jasper

Activities: Time in nature, Relaxation, Exercise, Time with loved ones

Day 1: I Love My Body

Goddess, your body was put on this Earth for JOY. Your senses are here to connect you with the curiosity of Source exploring and learning about itself. Your body was here to dance, to rest, to eat, to make love, to play, to learn, to connect, to heal, to nourish, to grow, and eventually to pass and become one with the Earth, providing soil for new life to emerge.

Your body started as an egg within your mother while in the womb within her mother. Your body is the result of thousands of generations of mothers, bleeding and gestating and birthing and nursing. Your body is the result of millions of years of evolution, fine-tuning your DNA into the perfect vessel for your soul. The Earth was formed from the stars, your body formed from the Earth. Your body has trillions of cells working together, pumping blood through your heart, air through your lungs, electricity through your nervous system, eliminating waste, protecting you from disease and illness. Your body is both a temple and a force of nature! How could it be anything but perfect?

We are born, and over the course of a few months, all of our senses become engaged and fine-tuned, and we are CURIOUS. We gaze at our mothers, at the world around us, in complete wonder and without judgment. Our bodies are tools we slowly learn to use. Look, I've discovered my hands! I've found my feet and I can put them in my mouth! I can clap my hands together and they make an amazing noise! I can crawl and explore the world around me! I can walk! I can run! I can DANCE!

But somewhere along the way, and it's very early for girls, we start to learn that our bodies are not for our sole enjoyment. That women's bodies are a commodity and are rarely "good enough" to earn our keep. That our bodies are for others' entertainment, enjoyment, and pleasure. That when our bodies grow and mature, they become both disgusting and enticing. We're touched when we don't want to be touched, we're judged when we don't want to be judged, and we're meant to take it all in with a smile.

We remove our body hair, we slather on lotions and potions full of unsavory chemicals, we damage our skin, we wear painful undergarments and torture our feet. Maybe we hide our bodies under layers of clothing so that we can keep something to and for ourselves. We diet, we starve, we binge and purge. We photoshop, we filter, we angle our bodies just so. It's all so... exhausting.

Queen, I am not saying that it's not OK to wear makeup, style your hair, take a selfie, get your nails done, be sexy, or anything else you damn well please. I'm just saying that you ADORN you for YOU. For YOUR pleasure. For your enjoyment and entertainment. To play. To send a message that you're a badass bitch or a bringer of JOY. Because you fucking love glitter and want to shine like your Inner Goddess. As the great Drag Queen RuPaul says, "We are all born naked and the rest is drag." The drag may as well be FUN!

Our bodies hold so much intelligence. When we are chronically stressed or are holding onto trauma, and let's be honest, ladies, we ALL have it, our minds and bodies disconnect. It can be difficult to know where your body is in space and to tune into its inner sensations. But when we commit to embodiment practices such as yoga, sports, dance, breathwork, body scan meditations, and more, we reconnect the mind and body. We notice that we are not just "thinking" with the mind, but with the pussy, the womb, the gut, and the heart as well. We ask these minds within questions and they provide us with answers. We feel embodied, alive, in the moment. We're able to ask our body what she needs and when she needs it. We tune into our animal body, and like a lioness on the plains of Africa, know what we instinctively need to thrive. We also connect to our Inner Goddess via the body, providing her with the intelligence and intuition to become our highest selves.

Our body is a fabulous and intelligent vehicle for exploration, learning, and dancing with the divine. Our curves mimic the mountains, our stretch marks the patterns in a leaf, our laugh lines ripples in glorious waters. Our bodies hold our story and our story is BEAUTIFUL.

As Ram Dass said, "Treat everyone like God in drag." And know that YOU are a goddess in drag. And your drag is FIERCE, Queen! You better WERK because it's only a short amount of time until we give this borrowed body back to Mama Gaia. Let's not waste it berating ourselves and instead spend it embracing ourselves!

Reflection:
Make a list of all of the limiting beliefs and negative thoughts you hold about your body. After you create the list, look at each belief, and next to it, write where this belief came from. Chances are, the belief that your body isn't perfect came from media, from family, from unenlightened partners, or from comparison. Now, write a positive affirmation to help rewire each limiting belief.

Example:
Limiting Belief: My skin is bumpy, red, wrinkled, and ugly.
Source: Photoshopped images from makeup ads of perfect skin.
Affirmation: My skin is beautiful and I embrace my pores, scars, lines, and bumps, because they tell my human story and my story is beautiful.

Embodiment Practice:
Give yourself a massage, starting at your feet and ending with your head. You can be clothed or nude. You can keep your setup simple, or use oils, light candles, and set a mood. As you knead, massage, and caress your body, repeat the mantra, "My body is mine. My body is sacred. My body is beautiful."

Day 2: I Move with Joy

Friend, are you moving that beautiful body of yours enough? When is the last time you danced? When is the last time you put your feet upon the Earth and just walked with no particular route or destination? Are you twerking? Chopping wood? Prancercising? How are you connecting your body to the freedom and the joy that is movement?

I remember being a small child and spinning, running, jumping, dancing, and playing without a watch telling me when or how to move, an app reminding me which muscle groups to work, or a social media influencer showing me her beautiful bum and how exactly to get it that way. (Spoiler alert, it's posing!)

My preferred method of movement from childhood through my early twenties was dance. Jazz, tap, ballet, lyrical, modern, give me it all! As a kid, I loved moving with my friends, performing, and just feeling myself and the music. Whenever anything else was going on in my life, I could set it aside and just dance my ass off, make goofy faces in the mirror, leap and spin until all there was, was my body and the music. In my teens, I started getting pretty good, and I was aiming to become professional. Unfortunately, I also had a pretty strong idea of what a professional dancer's body looked like and spiraled heavily into an eating disorder. The mirror was suddenly the enemy and so was my body.

When it came time for college, I had begun my initial healing journey but I was far from stable. Deciding to stay close to home, I accepted an academic scholarship at a nearby university and decided to major in dance. Unfortunately, the damage was done. I wasn't healthy enough to commit to dance or school and dropped out after three semesters.

Over the next few years, I did a lot of yoga and Pilates videos but without the structure and community of dance, and with the eating disorder still waxing and waning, I felt lost and very disconnected from my body. The most joyous movement was during nights out with my friends, dancing at clubs, whiskey and ginger ale in my hand.

At 27, when I moved home and really started to focus on my healing, I started yoga at a local community center. I couldn't believe how foreign my body felt, but after a few weeks, my dancer's muscle memory kicked in and it started feeling really amazing to move again.

I committed myself to the practice, going to local studios and eventually becoming a yoga teacher. I felt so strong, and practicing intentional movement helped me feel more in control of my mind and connected to my body. I even opened a donation-based yoga studio so I could create a place for people to move joyfully and be themselves in community.

In the past decade, I've also fallen in love with lifting weights, dancing for fun, hiking, kayaking, paddle boarding, and more. Now that I'm a full-time mom and it's difficult to go to the gym or to classes, I just listen to my body and my menstrual cycle, and move in whatever way feels satisfying.

Sister, I can't tell you how good it feels to just move my body for the sake of moving. It's not connected to weight loss, or perfecting an art, or anything else. Just good old-fashioned endorphins, longevity, and joy. My favorite is to put on some music and dance like a complete fool in my living room. Letting go of all the training and just letting go and being in joy.

Goddess, we were made to move! While it's in the masculine to sit, meditate, and become one with spirit, it's very much in the feminine to connect to Goddess through joyful and ecstatic movement. To lose ourselves in the bliss of using our bodies as prayers, as bridges to divine connection. To sway our hips and shimmy our shoulders and shake our asses. We don't have to look a certain way or dance or move for the pleasure or gaze of ANYONE but us and our Inner Goddess.

And when we dance together? We raise the vibration of the whole damn planet. We dance for joy. We dance for peace. We dance for the ecstasy available in the moment. We dance for us.

Reflection:
What is your favorite way to move your body? When do you feel most fluid? When do you feel most strong?

Embodiment Practice:
Choose a song that brings you joy and makes you want to dance. While you listen to it, let your body move in ways that feel straight-up silly. Throw all inhibitions out the window, forget about looking cool or sexy, shake your bum, pump your arms, make stupid faces, and throw in some silly vocalizations. Do it alone or invite a friend to join!

Day 3: I Self-Regulate

At age 27, I was at rock bottom. I had dropped out of school, was in over $100,000 in student loan debt, had even more debt from two hospitalizations and surgery, went through a really painful breakup, and was riddled with anxiety, depression, disordered eating and couldn't see any kind of happy future for myself. I felt exhausted, defeated, and hopeless. I just didn't understand why things that seemed so simple to others were so damn difficult for me. I had been living in Tampa, Florida for the last three years, in Chicago four years before that. Running from a problem that followed me wherever I went. I knew it in my heart that it was time to move back home to Kansas City, Missouri, something I truly never thought I would do. I sold and gave away most of my belongings, packed up my Toyota Corolla with what was left, stuffed my fluffy cat Bowie into the car, and started my journey home.

My parents and family received me with open arms. I moved in with my brother and his wife to be a live-in nanny for awhile while I sorted my shit out. I started taking yoga classes regularly and my folks offered to pay for an experimental treatment called Neurofeedback. Although they weren't big on alternative healing, their friend's child had seen great success with Neurofeedback in healing depression and addiction, so they had some hope for me.

In my first appointment, my practitioner, Laura, hooked electrodes up to my head to measure my brain waves while I watched a simple graphic on a screen. She had me assess how I was feeling in the moment. "Normal," I thought, but she showed me how my nervous system was, in fact, in fight or flight mode. If this was my "normal", my nervous system was in fight or flight almost ALL THE TIME. No wonder it was so difficult for me to function! Over the course of 30 sessions, the therapy (which I still don't totally understand how looking at these simple video-game-like graphics and measuring my brain waves worked) actually worked quite brilliantly! She also introduced me to HeartMath and taught me how to regulate my heartbeat with my breath in order to regulate my nervous system. Game-changer!

Over the years, I have been increasingly interested in the trauma-response and how to create safety and resiliency in my body and to help others do the same. I've become a trauma-aware yoga teacher and facilitate yoga teacher trainings that incorporate trauma sensitivity. I have learned SO MUCH and I wish the whole world knew so we can stop traumatizing each other.

As human beings, our nervous systems have not caught up to modern life. We were wired to respond to danger (think a bear attack) by either fighting back, running away, freezing, or befriending the bear. These are known as fight, flight, freeze, and fawn. In modern times, although we might experience major trauma, many of our stressors are not of the type that threaten our immediate physical safety. However, our bodies still respond as if the bear is attacking.

For instance, have you ever received a text message that triggers you? What is your response? To fight back immediately? To ghost the person? To feel paralyzed, not knowing how to respond? Or maybe to immediately try and remedy the situation by people-pleasing and apologizing? You're not in "danger", nevertheless, your pulse still quickens, your pupils dilate, you start to sweat, and your digestion slows.

These trauma responses, over time, become "stuck" in the body and we end up in states where we are constantly just trying to survive. Furthermore, we subconsciously seek out situations that simulate our trauma again and again, and then pass the unhealed trauma along to our children.

This might feel like a lot, but there is hope. The good news is that there are ways to discharge the trauma and heal our nervous systems. If you have acute or complex trauma, I highly recommend seeing a professional therapist, trauma-informed yoga teacher, EMDR practitioner, or somatic therapist.

It's extremely important to get into the body, to be embodied, to self-regulate and heal. Have you ever noticed how a dog shakes after a traumatic event? They are literally discharging the trauma from their bodies. Have you noticed that many indigenous cultures dance together in ceremony? They are discharging trauma communally. In "civilized" society, we are so disconnected from our bodies and community that we have lost the ancestral wisdom of our foremothers and fathers. We are a traumatized society, ya'll, and it's time to shake it out.

Yoga, dancing, shamanic shaking, vocal activations, breathwork, getting into nature, laughing, playing, being in conscious community, and more, are all embodiment practices to connect you with your sacred vessel and regulate your nervous system. Anything that helps you release energy, helps you feel safe in your body, encourages autonomy and resets your internal rhythm is the medicine needed to break trauma cycles, and to stop surviving and start thriving!

Furthermore, while we can do our own work, we do not exist individually in a vacuum and it is vital that ALL of our businesses, governments, systems, and structures hop on the trauma-informed train to create global peace, joy, and FREEDOM from suffering! We thrive when we ALL thrive together!

Queen, this is the work of the sacred feminine. You DESERVE to feel safe in your beautiful body. You deserve to feel connected to her, to Gaia, to your sisters. You deserve to thrive. Free yourself, and in turn, free us all from the bondage of trauma!

Reflection:
How do you normally react to a trigger? Do you fight, run, freeze, or fawn? What practices help you feel most calm, centered, and regulated? Could you benefit from a professional trauma specialist?

Embodiment Practice:
A great way to regulate your nervous system is through diaphragmatic breathing. The diaphragm, which is under your ribs and works as a bellows, is one of the primary muscles that fills and empties the lungs with air. Many adults do not fully utilize this muscle due to trauma and chronic stress. If this is new to you, go slow and be gentle with yourself. Conscious breathing can take some practice in order to feel comfortable.

Place your hand on your belly. As you breathe in deeply, feel your belly expand outward into your hand. As you exhale as completely as possible, feel your belly and hand soften toward your spine. Repeat 10 times and notice how you feel.

Day 4: I Love My Inner Child

Sister, is your Inner Child begging to be acknowledged? Does she need to dance? To cry? To delight in the joy and mystery of life? To dream? To heal? Does she need to be rocked, sung to, and held? To be mothered? Does she need to know it wasn't her fault? Does she need to know she was perfectly made?

Your Inner Child and your Inner Goddess are intrinsically linked. You as a child came into this world fully realized, holy, fresh from her heavenly home. She is the higher self, the goddess. But time, cultural conditioning, and worldly weariness inevitably crept in. Told her who she should be. Made her hide the parts of herself that didn't fit in. Told her she's too little or too much. That being her isn't safe. As she grew from child to adult, she was shrouded by layers of limiting beliefs, pain, protection, and masks.

By acknowledging and loving on your Inner Child, you are excavating these layers that aren't truly **you**. As you mother your innocence with compassion, you are inviting in deep healing, penetrating the core of your being, inviting the Inner Child/Goddess to break free and unapologetically come to the surface.

I wrote this letter to my Inner Child to invite her to shine. To heal. To integrate into my being. Below in the Reflection, I invite you to do the same.

Dear Inner Child,

I love you. Please forgive me for forgetting you. For detaching from you. For abandoning you for adulthood.

If I could, I would hold you, as I do my own daughter, and remind you that you are perfect, you are love incarnate, and that nothing could ever tarnish your bright spirit.

The world can be a tough place. Judgment, criticism, social norms, old systems, people who love us but are hurt, people who don't understand us, companies that just want to make money from us, those who don't see our humanity, and a traumatized society can make us forget our magic. They can make us believe that we have to trade the magic of childhood for the responsibility of adulthood. That play is frivolous and dreams are meant to die.

But magic is real and you hold it in every cell of your being. Your voice, your heart, your body, your breath are pure magic. Your curiosity, your joy, your perspective, your gifts, are magic. No one can take that from you.

Little one, sometimes clouds can obscure the Sun, but the Sun is always there. So too is your inner light. When you are sad, when you are lonely, when you are scared, when you are misunderstood, when life seems so unfair, when your emotions are so big no one can hold them, your light is still there, bright as the Sun.

You are strong. You are beautiful. You are kind. You are infinitely creative. You are so very fun. You are deep. You are interesting. You are tenacious. You are gifted. You are more powerful than you know. You are worthy. You are enough. You are unique. Your body is yours. Your mind is yours. Your spirit is yours. And you get to choose how and when to share them and who to share them with.

I see you. I embrace you. I heal your wounds. I love you.

Life will get tough. And you'll forget yourself again and again. Life is not a Disney Movie. You don't have to wait for a prince to save you and never have to give up parts of yourself to be victorious. You are the heroine of your own journey. You are your own savior. You are the chosen one.

Little one, use your JOY as a compass. Let it lead you on your dharmic path. By following your joy, by being you, others will be invited to do the same. Little one, there will be those who are triggered by your joy. Who want to squash it. Who make you feel wrong for it. But they are triggered because they are so disconnected from their own joy that seeing someone else's just reminds them of their deep despair. It is not your job to shrink for these people. It is your job to shine despite and because of them. We are all connected, and by you being in joy, you are raising the frequency of this planet. Those in the darkness will follow in their own time. It's inevitable.

Dear little one, I love you. When you can't see the light, I ask you to have faith in yourself. To know that brighter days are coming. To know that as you are older, you'll remember who you truly are and why you're here. That your older self will embrace you and lead with you. That you are exactly the medicine she needs and the world needs.

Before your mother birthed you, you saw the possibilities of your life ahead and entered a sacred contract to fulfill your *dharma*. Every single thing you have experienced is to enrich, inform, and expand you. Your whole life is for you. You are here to learn, grow, and raise the vibration of the whole planet. This world needs you. It needs you, your gifts, it needs your voice, it needs your bravery, and it needs it NOW.

Little one, thank you. Thank you for teaching me, for healing me, for being me. I integrate you into my whole self, and together, we know who we are. Divine light. Pure joy. Goddess incarnate.

Love,

Me

Reflection:
Take a few moments to go inward and connect with your Inner Child. Visualize her surrounded by an aura of love and compassion. Then, write a letter to your Inner Child. Allow yourself to flow freely and to accept any emotions that arise in the process.

Embodiment Practice:
What activity brought you the most joy as a child? Playing outside? Singing? Listening to music? Schedule in 20 minutes today for your favorite childhood activity. Allow yourself to play without regard to any specific outcome. Are you making art? Do it for fun and not for the result. Allow yourself to throw perfectionism out the window and simply enjoy being in the moment.

Day 5: I Am Home

Is your home a sacred space or is it a reflection of inner chaos?

To be honest, I never really understood the connection between a tidy, peaceful home and a calm mind until well into adulthood.

When I was a kid, it always seemed as though a tornado had made its way across my bedroom. Clothes everywhere. Art projects askew. Forgotten collections of random objects. It was chaos and I didn't really seem to notice or care. I once even found a long-lost bottle of Snapple that had fermented, sounding like a bottle of champagne once opened. Gross, I know.

My room became a battle of wills between myself and my father. We were in the same unhealthy cycle for years. I would casually allow my room to become a hazard-zone. Every few weeks he would enter my room, see the disaster, and go absolutely berserk, yelling at me for the way I was neglecting our house and treating my belongings like trash, screaming, "Get your head out of your butt and clean it up!" I would cry and panic, clean my room, and afterward he would apologize to me for losing his temper. I would then slowly allow my room to go back to its chaotic state while riding on low-key constant anxiety for the inevitable outcome of my carelessness.

My father came from strict parents and served in the Air Force before he and my mother were married. He had three children and a high stress job, and I just so happened to trigger the shit out of him with my mess. One time, when I was maybe 12, I hadn't done my laundry in quite some time and the house was running low on towels. He went into my closet and pulled out 21 towels, yelling and counting them one by one, me crumbling and sobbing in shame. To this day, he jokes about this incident, calling it the "21 towel salute", but in the moment, our nervous systems were both going off like tornado sirens, begging us to pause and take shelter.

Up until recently, I didn't quite understand why I couldn't seem to get this particular thing right. Why I was such a mess. I was an A student, "gifted" in fact. I was in Sunday school every week, a kind friend, highly creative, wise beyond my years, a talented singer and dancer, and a really, really good girl. I guess holding onto all of that achievement, the pressure boiling over, something had to give. First it was my room, then it was my eating disorder, anxiety, and depression.

I've since learned that gifted children have brains that work almost too quickly, and since school often come easily, they never develop appropriate time management and organizational skills. Parents don't often understand because their child is so intelligent, shouldn't those qualities come innately? This hit home for me. It really wasn't until my late 20s/early 30s that I started seeking resources to help me learn these skills I missed and now so desperately needed.

After moving out on my own, and filling my homes with creative projects and oddball thrift store finds, I was able to keep it together a bit better for roommates, having guests over in my own space, and eventually for sharing space with my husband. But tidiness still didn't quite click. I never felt rooted anywhere (I've lived in 14 homes in 20 years!), and I still hadn't felt quite at home within myself. My home always verged on reflecting the inner chaos I felt.

When I began a formal meditation practice, I could truly see for the first time the utter chaos in my mind. The thoughts just going, going, going all the time, in the past, in the future, anywhere but here. The more I practiced, the calmer my mind became.

I've had the privilege of visiting many retreat centers in the last decade and one thing they all have in common is tranquility cultivated by intentional and clean spaces. It was on a trip to my yoga school in Spain where it finally really clicked with me that I deeply desired for my home to be a sacred space and that my outer world can help or hinder my inner peace. Tidy home, tidy mind.

Since then, I have been drawn to neutral colors, organized spaces, and a home with a good flow. In my efforts to create a tranquil home, however, I've caught myself picking up after my husband, grumbling to myself about his untidiness. Or being so caught up in an area of the home being untidy or disorganized, that I have a hard time being present until it gets done. Oh, how the tables have turned and my compassion for my father has grown.

But in motherhood, as my perspective has widened and changed, I've had to sometimes choose presence and play over immediate tidiness. In fact, as I write this, I'm in my living room of our "forever home" with toys strewn about instead of in their tidy cubbies, evidence of my daughter's creativity and exploration. And I'm OK with that and know it will be easy to tidy when I've closed my laptop. And if it doesn't get done? I can still manage my mind and nervous system.

What I have learned is that my home is my sanctuary. It doesn't have to be perfect, but it does need to reflect my values. I tidy my home not just in search of an ideal Instagram-worthy aesthetic but in sacred service to myself and my family. It's a spiritual practice. Furthermore, a tidy home does not equal a happy home (although it can help!). What's important to me is that my home is high vibe and that it's a safe place for my family to be themselves, love each other, and grow. We need not clutter it with harsh words or actions.

I also love having dedicated sacred spaces, or altars throughout my home. Little treasure stations with plants, crystals, deities, oracle cards, lavender smudge, family pictures, you name it. I love having these reminders around me to pause, be grateful, and know that I'm holding within me magic.

Ultimately, although it is cliche, home is where the heart is. Whether or not you currently have a physical space that is representative of your values, your true home is within. Your heart is an altar, your Solar Plexus its flame, your womb a cauldron, and your yoni a sacred portal. When feeling lost, lonely, in chaos, or maybe you're holding on too tight to being a "good girl" you can tune into your heart, offering her your deepest prayers, and remember who you truly are.

Reflection:
Do you feel a correlation between the state of your home and the state of your mind? What is "home" to you? When do you feel most at home?

Embodiment Practice:
Find a small space in your home to create a sacred altar. This can be a shelf, table, dresser, cubby, or any other small and safe space in an area you frequent. Adorn the space with things that remind you of beauty, connection, and spirit. Examples might be crystals, herbs, candles, sacred texts, oracle cards, affirmation, pictures, and flowers. It can be very simple, or very elaborate. Return to this space to meditate, pray, connect, or even to journey through this book. If you already have an altar, take a few minutes to tidy, freshen, and rearrange it.

Day 6: I Am Abundant

Are you living in abundance? Or does the thought of money make you want to run the other way?

Many of us are living in scarcity. And there is plenty of reason for it! We live in a world where a few people have many billions of dollars and others are dying from starvation. In the US, which is supposed to be a "first world" country, education and medical care can put us into massive debt. Where housing costs are rising and the stock market is tanking. Maybe you grew up in poverty and it's wired your system for scarcity. Maybe your parents mismanaged, overspent, or held on too tight to their money. Maybe you scroll through Instagram and see influencer after influencer flaunting designer bags and flashy cars while shilling over-the-top expensive skincare. Maybe society's messaging has taught us that if we can just get to a certain income level, our problems will be solved. It feels like there is never enough and certainly not enough for us to truly thrive.

Read the last paragraph again and notice the sensations in your body as you take it in. Where do you feel scarcity in your body? Where does this money fear lie?

I know this exact feeling. For me, it's a pit in my stomach and a clenching of my throat. It's a feeling of desperation and despair. Of worthlessness.

On one of our first dates, my now husband, Arthur, took me out to eat. I ordered something small and cheap, my habit as I was living on a tight budget. He kept reaching over and taking food off of my plate to taste and I found myself at first feeling uncomfortable, and soon enough, angry. He could tell something was wrong and when I told him what was up, he said, "Well, we can just order more."

And honestly, that blew my mind. At that time, age 24 and living in Tampa, Florida, I was in over $100,000 in student debt, was about to drop out of school, even though I was so close to graduating, because I couldn't manage my anxiety and depression. I was making $10 an hour at a fun boutique job that wasn't exactly a long-term career plan. And I blew what little expendable income I had on weed, going out dancing, and vintage clothing. I looked fabulous but I had a constant pit in my stomach and tightness in my throat, feeling the scarcity and shoving my money fears deep down and numbing them away.

A few nights before the date, I had very little food in the house. I was opening up a box of couscous for dinner. I miscalculated the force needed to open it, the box ripped open, and teeny tiny grains of couscous went everywhere. I had a full-on meltdown.

So someone "stealing" off of my plate (even though he was paying) was highly triggering. And I thought, "We can just order more?"

Around the same time, desperate to change my mindset and story around money, I discovered Lakshmi, the Hindu Goddess of material and spiritual wealth and fortune. I felt connected to her energy: serene, unapologetic, and luxurious. I deeply wanted to embody her essence. I listened to recordings and chanted along to *Om Shree Maha Lakshmiyei Swaha*, a Sanskrit mantra in adoration of the Goddess. I would chant it in times where I felt scarcity and lack, imagining myself as her and inviting in her abundant currency of wealth.

Four years later, Arthur and I married. Being highly affected by the recession and housing crisis of 2008, he had just declared bankruptcy, short sold his home in Florida and chased me to Kansas City where we started our life together. We had nothing but debt between us, but we found a place to live (even though almost no one would rent to us) and hustled through self-employment that wasn't exactly soul purposeful.

He was freelancing doing SEO and website building, and I was nannying. Although we didn't have much, life always felt abundant together. We had fun with family, made the most of our apartment, made good friends and cooked good food, and started building a life from less than scratch. Our love and support for one another and a feeling of "nothing left to lose" put us in the vibration of abundance. The sick feeling in my stomach started to relax and I started believing in my worth, in our worth.

In the next few years as I healed and grew, I became a yoga teacher, opened my own yoga studio, started leading international retreats, started my own yoga teacher training, and building more and more self-worth, confidence and abundance. Alongside me, Arthur opened a taco restaurant that was featured on Food Network and is now one of the busiest restaurants in Kansas City, which has an impressive food scene. We went from living in that apartment to now owning an older but comfortable home on a nearby lake where we can relax and renovate in our own time. I'm still working on raising my credit score and paying off my debt, but I do not hold the same energy or emotional attachment around it anymore. Just because I have financial debt does not mean I have a debt of self-worth. I am so proud of how far I have come and know my potential is infinite.

In my healing journey, I have had to completely rewrite my internal stories around money and abundance. I realized that abundance isn't material wealth, but a feeling of joy, gratitude, and giving. Abundance is a whole damn vibe and the more you feel it, the more you attract. Do what you need to do to get into the vibe. Get your hands in the dirt to grow food, light your good candles, use your good skin care, make conscious purchases, give money freely, laugh often, and enjoy your body. Get rid of any belongings, expenses, or people who don't spark joy, and revel in your gratitude for your curated life.

Abundance isn't consumerism or having a ton of things, it's having more than enough and sharing the wealth. It's surrounding ourselves with experiences, and people who add value to our lives. It's about quality, not quantity.

The truth of our reality is that it IS abundant. Look at Mother Earth. She is perfect and provides everything we need. Plants for medicine and food, clean water for drinking and bathing, trees and earth to build shelter, and so much more. Look at our Universe. It's Infinitely expansive and anything is truly possible within it. Look at your heart, Queen. Maybe there are walls around it but its true nature is boundless. Look at love, it's unconditional.

Goddess, you are capable of ANYTHING and EVERYTHING. Money is simply a currency (or current) and it flows through you with abundance and ease. You deserve to know your worth, to feel your worth, to embody your worth. You deserve not a pit in your stomach, but a calm nervous system, a fertile womb, and an open heart. You are a magnificent queen and you are ABUNDANT.

Reflection:
When do you feel most abundant? What thoughts, habits, or belongings can you release to feel more in the vibration of abundance?

Embodiment Practice:
Practice Japa Meditation, a technique where you repeat a sacred mantra either silently or aloud. I invite you to chant, *"Om Shree Maha Lakshmiyei Swaha,"* (pronounced OH-m SHREE MAH-hah LAHK-shmee-YAY SWAH-hah) 108 times either silently or out loud. You can use your

fingers, or you can use mala beads if you have any on hand. You can also search for a recording of the chant and simply listen. While chanting or listening, imagine yourself embodying the essence of prosperity. Feel it in your body. And then notice how your energy shifts.

Day 7: I Connect to Mama Earth

Sister, do you allow yourself to receive the abundant gifts from Mother Earth? When you feel scattered, anxious, scared or unclear, she is here to cradle you in her arms and connect you to your body. She is here to soothe you, ground you, and to help you remember the magic of the present moment. She is here to remind you that you are a part of everything and that everyone is interconnected. She whispers to go at your own pace. She reveals to you that wherever you are, you are home.

When I am meditating on Mother Earth, there are a few beautiful memories my mind likes to bathe in.

When I worked at the vintage shop, my boss took all of the staff to her home in the mountains of North Carolina. I was healing from ovarian surgery. Unable to join in many of the more active adventures, I spent much of my time sitting by a creek on the property. Shaded by gorgeous trees, in just my own company. Cool mountain air on my skin. I sat by the creek for hours, staring at the flowing crystal clear water. Glittering rocks in the creek bed glinting with glimpses of Sun through the trees. I was in pain, but the longer I observed the rolling waters, the more they washed away the ache in my womb and troubles of my mind.

In the chaos of my mid-twenties, amidst heartache and loss, I traveled alone to a secluded beach. I played and swam in the warm crystalline waters of the Gulf, pretending to be a mermaid. While I twirled, flipped, and floated in the gentle safety waves, I forgot everything but the moment itself.

Walking along a secluded beach during my yoga teacher training in Costa Rica. Looking up to see a migration of brilliant blue butterflies. Their mass taking up the whole sky and stretching to the horizon. My breath caught in my throat in pure awe.

When I was first building my business and feeling the stress of it all, sitting on my parents' dock for hours at the Lake of the Ozarks. Staring at the water. Watching my husband kayaking in the distance. Meditating on the reflection of the water on the dock roof. An Ephemeral dance of light. Calm washing over me.

In Bali with a group of women as I was leading yoga on a retreat. We awoke at 2am to climb Mount Batur in the dark, summiting at Sunrise. The effort and connection with the rocky terrain leading to the reward of Mother Earth's magical show of colors, mist, and light. On the descent, we meditated in a cave, giving gratitude for the moment, our strength and smallness, and the magnificence of spirit and nature.

In Guatemala, waking up to the view of beautiful volcanoes and the waters of Lake Atitlán, flowers everywhere.

In Greece, hiking through wild herbs and flora, the Mediterranean glinting in the distance on the island of Amorgos.

In India, hiking alone through the Beatles Ashram in Rishikesh. Abandoned meditation caves overgrown with trees and vines. The bustling city and the river Ganga Ma in the distance.

On the lawn of The Nelson-Atkins Museum of Art in Kansas City, teaching yoga and soaking up rare Sun on an early March day, beautiful folks breathing and moving before me.

A few days ago, sitting on my deck with my daughter, I looked up in the sky to see a bald eagle swooping close by, descending to the water with perfect precision, catching a fish in its talons and flying away.

Even writing this, my little lake right out the window, birds visiting my birdfeeder, the trees holding tiny buds with their first promises of Spring.

I am forever grateful for Mother Earth and her selfless abundance. All elements working perfectly together in harmony, effortlessly working toward homeostasis at all times, birthing us, sustaining us, and providing home to our bodies when we pass. She is the ultimate mother.

Sisters, there is a reason that humans worshipped the Earth and the Goddess for many millennia before the rise of Patriarchal religions. Because when we live in harmony with her, we live in harmony with ourselves. When we worship her seasons, her cycles, her mystery, her magic, we know that we are a part of her, thus holding her magic. She gives to us and we promise to be a grateful steward of our home, preserving her for our descendants, letting her be in her wildness, giving Mama Earth her sovereignty, and giving of ourselves back to her when it's time.

Sisters, it is no mistake that as we distance ourselves from the sacred feminine, we distance ourselves from a harmonious relationship with Mama Gaia. As we humans abuse our mother, we abuse ourselves. As the landfills fill, as we take her oil, as we rape her forests and toxify her air, the Goddess self-corrects. Let's remember that as long as our Sun shines, Mama Earth will be just fine. It's humanity who is in danger.

Queens, let us rise up. Let us care for Mama. Let us be good ancestors. Let us breathe in the abundance of Earth while leaving her better than we found her. We are her daughters, her tenants, her congregation. Let us treat her, and in turn ourselves, with the utmost reverence. Let us know that our bodies, borrowed from her, are temples. Let us place our bare feet upon her as a prayer. Let us bathe in her waters as purification. Let us take the deepest of breaths as a mantra. Let us dance upon her as worship. Let us be with her in the ecstasy of existence.

Reflection:
Make a list of your most soothing memories in Nature. When have you been most in awe of Mother Earth?

Embodiment Practice:
Weather and environment permitting, take off your shoes and walk, dance, stand, or practice yoga barefoot on the Earth. This practice known as "Earthing" is said to tap into the electrical energy of the Earth, which reduces stress, inflammation, and pain. If this is not an option for you, find a crystal or rock, hold it in your hands, and imagine yourself receiving healing energy from Mama Earth.

Week Two

The Sacral Chakra

We continue our journey this week in the feminine, flowing, and powerfully creative, Sacral Chakra, or *Swadhisthana*. Located just below the navel, this chakra tethers us to the cycles of the moon, invites our feminine side to revel in pleasure, and connects us to the power of creation. As we dive into our deep inner waters, we are asked to feel all our big emotions, unleash our sensuality, embrace our relationships, and dance in our feminine creative power.

I invite you to take a moment and place your hands on your sacred womb. Whether or not you have a physical womb, you can still connect to the powerful creative energy within your being. Take several deep breaths and focus your energy and attention on the Sacral Chakra. See it spinning, an orange six-petaled flower. Imagine it connecting you to all the waters of the Earth, as well as your waters within. See it pulsing with life-force, pleasure, and potential. Feel it connecting you to your deepest emotions, your deepest desires, your untamed wildness. You might fill the chakra with its sacred sound, *Vam*, by chanting it deeply three times. Then release with a breath in through the nose, and out through the mouth.

Many people, including myself, hold deep wounding in this chakra. Consider the Sacral Chakra, with its wild and feminine nature, in direct resistance to a linear Patriarchal world. Where we are expected to conform to gender, sexual, racial, and class norms. Where we have to work like we don't bleed. Where we sacrifice our pleasure and contain our emotions. Where we are expected to perform sexuality but never actually own it. Where we sacrifice our souls at the altar of consumerism and survival. The Sacral Chakra is a straight-up rebel and she is longing to be healed, uncaged, and set free. This process does not happen overnight, so I invite you to be gentle with yourself, to embrace small victories, and to accept wherever you are in this process of embodying your Inner Goddess.

Sacral Chakra (*Swadhisthana*)
Location: The lower belly and lumbar spine. The physical or energetic womb.
Energy: Creativity, Emotions, Pleasure, Sensuality, Relationships
Color: Orange
Sacred Sound: Vam
Element: Water
Overactive Chakra Symptoms: Drama. Sexual Overindulgence. Inability to delay pleasure.

Underactive Chakra Symptoms: Depression. Creative blocks. Disconnect from sensuality and receiving.

When in Balance: We are in tune with our senses and pleasure. We live in a state of effortless flow. We are able to receive and relax. We are creative, curious, and playful. We embrace life's cyclical nature.

Connect to the Sacral Chakra with:

Food: Oranges, Carrots, Peaches

Scents: Cardamom, Sweet Orange, Ylang

Crystals: Carnelian, Tiger's Eye, Sunstone

Activities: Art, Swimming, Baths, Play, Sex, Self-pleasure

Day 8: I Live in Flow

Are you living your life in flow?

Before my husband and I decided to conceive our daughter, Gemma, I felt like my life was in tidy order. Since tidiness was really never in my nature, the amount of work I had put into learning time management and organizational skills so I could thrive as an entrepreneur was impressive. I had structured my days so I could concentrate on my well-being while also creating at a high-level. I crafted a strong structure that I could flow and play within, a perfect balance of masculine and feminine. It seemed to be the ideal time to finally call my baby in.

In March of 2020, my husband and I conceived our baby just as the world was shutting down due to COVID-19. Instantly, the rules had changed and my perfect plan suddenly seemed a bit shaky. I had to quickly shift my yoga studio to a virtual platform and change my routines to support a pregnancy in the first trimester that required me to slow waaaay down.

Over the coming months I had to keep shifting my business to deal with changing guidelines while trying to lead a burned-out team and class of yoga teacher trainees. I mostly stayed at home, and while I felt in peace and in love with my pregnancy, the world was in chaos. The only thing I could control was my home and trying to keep my vessel healthy for the baby. I couldn't hold onto any routine too tightly, knowing it could have to change any minute.

After Gemma was born in November 2020, postpartum life, especially mid-pandemic, was one the most difficult experiences of my life. It felt like every bit of routine and structure I had previously thrived on had to be thrown out the window. I barely slept, my hormones were going crazy, I was obsessed with keeping my little one safe, and I couldn't even go to the bathroom, take a shower, make food, or fill a water bottle without help. And help was scarce due to the pandemic and my husband having to return to work so quickly. I couldn't do yoga or meditate or lift weights or any of the other self-care routines I had so heavily relied on. I felt thrown out to sea, grasping for control and safety where I could find it.

I promised Gemma I will always be the mother she needs and it turned out that she needed a high level of co-regulation, especially for the first year. She wouldn't sleep in a crib, didn't want to be put down, and wouldn't take a bottle or pacifier. I wore her, contact napped, co-slept, and exclusively nursed. Don't get me wrong, it was also a complete JOY, but I went from being a 36-year-old free-spirited woman to a 24/7 attachment mama. My mind was constantly on baby, my heart was expansive, and my emotions all over the place. I couldn't even imagine being anything ELSE but Mama, let alone take the reins back on my business, be creative, and be in my full *dharma*.

Life felt very out of my control and I had to surrender to the process of transforming from maiden to mother. I had to release expectations, let go of what worked for me in the past, figure out brand new rhythms with my new sweet baby, and trust that things might become easier in the future. The more I let go of expectations and found joy in the moment, and the more faith I had in the future, the more ease I found in my body and in the role of Mother.

Now, life with a toddler has a new rhythm and routine. Time has helped me feel more integrated and balanced, and I've stepped more fully into this new identity. Every day as a mama, teacher, and business owner has a flow. It's slower and messier than "before baby" but taking pauses between tasks to sing *Row, Row, Row Your Boat* at her request makes this time of my life that much sweeter.

Life is a dance between surrender and control, and the sweet spot in the middle is flow. This is actually a neurological process in the brain. The two hemispheres, right and left, need to work in harmony to achieve ease and flow. The right brain, creative and expressive, when out of balance leads to chaos. The left brain, logical and structured, when out of balance leads to rigidity. The path of flow is like a river flowing between the two and it's dangerous to veer off to either side and hit the riverbank.

When life brings big changes, we fear chaos and cling to rigidity. When life feels confining, we fear being trapped in rigidity and throw ourselves to chaos. However, the flow of the sacred feminine comes when we release attachment to the way things "ought to be", roll with life's inevitable changes, are present with what is right now, and when we keep our vessels (mind, body, and heart) strong and sound. When we row, row, row the boat gently down the stream, and do it with joy and faith, we align with the effortless flow of the Goddess.

Reflection:
What does your daily routine look like? Do you have a structure or schedule that leaves space for creativity, inspiration, and spontaneity? Could your days use more structure or more freedom?

Embodiment Practice:
Nadi Shodhana, or Alternate Nostril Breathing, a yogic breathwork technique, is said to balance the hemispheres of the brain and balance masculine and feminine. It is an excellent remedy to shift your energy, whether in chaos or rigidity, into a state of flow. Find *Vishnu Mudra* in the right hand by folding the index finger and middle finger

into the palm. Take the hand up to the nose, the thumb gently resting on the right nostril, and ring and pinky fingers resting on the left nostril. Plug the left nostril and inhale deeply through the right nostril. Then plug the right nostril and exhale fully out the left side. Breathe deeply through left, exhale through right. Inhale right, then exhale left. Continue for several rounds until you feel more regulated and at peace.

Day 9: I Embrace My Emotions

Do you embrace or run from your emotions?

One day, in the midst of my healing journey, I was feeling extremely frustrated. I wanted to heal, I wanted to befriend myself, I wanted to be happy, I wanted to love my life. I had moved back to my hometown, tried therapy, was practicing yoga, married to the love of my life. I couldn't figure out why I still couldn't stand my own company.

Like any millennial, I searched the great oracle, Google, for answers. I wasn't exactly sure even what to search. "Why am I so… " I drew a blank.

And then it hit me, "Why do I HATE myself?" I felt pathetic, but hey, maybe I'd find some answers.

I recently found a school assignment from age 6. I drew pictures on each page of me doing happy activities and captioned them as things I do each day of the week. On Monday, I go to school. On Tuesday, I go to singing class. And so on. I flipped to the back of the notebook to see in angry 6-year-old scrawl, "I HATE MYSELF." Ah, so I have a history with this.

I was a very emotional kid. Extremely bright and happy, extremely in touch with the sadness and anger too. I thought I was destined to be an actress, and emotions were my medium. When I'd get in trouble, I'd slam the door of my room, shove my face into a pillow and scream at the top of my lungs. I'd cry and snot all over. I'd tear things up. And then the storm would pass and I'd go on to happily play with my toys.

At some point, I received the message that this wasn't OK, and that I needed to embrace positive emotions, or even turn my emotions off, while putting aside the negative. That's maturity. One time, my mom told me that my dad would respect me more if I "took it like a man" when he yelled at me, so I had to train myself to look him in the eye and sit there calmly while being scolded. I knew that to be respected in this world, only showing certain emotions is OK.

Fast forward 20+ years to my google search. I scrolled through the results and happened upon an article about "Highly Sensitive People" or "HSPs". My jaw literally dropped as I read. Highly sensitive people FEEL intensely. Their senses are heightened. Emotions are visceral. They can easily be overwhelmed by the sensory experience of modern life. Overuse of technology, exposure to violence as entertainment, loud music with violent words, school and job that don't give a fuck what you're going through as long as you show up and be productive, lack of respect for and awareness of mental health, and treating people as consumers. These cultural qualities are HELL for an HSP. "Oh my God," I thought. "This is ME!"

Highly sensitive people make up about 15-20% of the population. They thrive well in cultures that value the more feminine traits of flow, intuition, subtlety, and quiet intelligence. In cultures, such as the US, they tend to drown in hyper-competitive, individualistic, power-praising masculinity.

I realized, I don't hate myself, I just haven't fully understood myself. That my hypersensitivity, while not feeling like an asset in my culture and the systems within it, is actually a SUPER POWER **if** I'm able to create a life that allows me to embrace sacred self-care, work at my own pace, find my own tribe, and use the gifts I was given to heal myself and help uplift humanity.

This really sparked my journey to become a yoga teacher and embrace the gifts I've been given. In my field, my sensitivity has been embraced, and with good self-regulation tools, I've been able to feel my emotions and transmute them.

The more we run from or shove down our emotions, the more potent they become in our bodies and the more likely they are going to come out in inappropriate ways or go inward and implode. I've always been an imploder. When I learned it wasn't safe or respected to show my emotions, I learned to shove them down until they turn into self-hate, depression, eating disorders, and addiction.

But, baby, you've got to feel to heal. You've got to let yourself feel emotions fully as they arise. Sit with them. Befriend them. Invite them into the sacred pause with you. Cry with them. Scream with them. Take breaks when they become too much, but return when you are ready. They want to be acknowledged. And the more we do this, the more easily they release from our system. We don't need to hide from the monsters in the closet, we need to open the door and invite them for tea.

When my baby girl has big feelings, I've learned to hold space for her as she lets them come. To be a calm witness and to nurture when needed. It is my hope that this is what we can all do for ourselves and our emotions.

Goddess, your emotions are beautiful. Your laughter, your tears, your cries are beautiful. Feel them, embrace them, thank them for what they are here to teach you, and let them go. And if you feel very, very deeply and tap into others' emotions as well, know that this is a superpower. Your heart is so big and so open. You can take all these emotions in, and instead of letting them harm you, your powerful heart can TRANSMUTE them all to love. To the very highest vibration for yourself and for all beings. This is within you. But only if you're brave enough to feel.

Reflection:

Do you allow yourself to feel your feelings? When you avoid big emotions, do you implode or explode? Do you feel ready to befriend your emotions?

Embodiment Practice:

Pause for a few moments and notice what you are feeling. What emotions are most at surface and what emotions are buried underneath? Notice where you feel your emotions in your body. Now, it's time to dance it out! Pick a song, joyful, angry, emo, whatever matches your innermost emotions. Play the song and dance it out! Don't worry about looking good or doing things "right". Let the music move your body and let your energy flow.

Day 10: I Cycle like the Moon

When I was in kindergarten, the teacher, Mrs. Hocker, asked the class if we knew what a period was. Being precocious, I raised my hand proudly and answered, "It's something that a mommy has!" The teacher, dumbfounded, moved right along to talk about punctuation. I was embarrassed but didn't know why. Oof.

I remember my mom grumbling about her "period" and "that time of the month" and feeling a little mystified and frightened by the wonders of womanhood.

At age 13, between grades 7 and 8, my dad took me shopping to get a required one-piece bathing suit for church camp. When changing, I noticed something in my underwear and thought maybe I had pooped my pants. When I got home to the bathroom, I noticed distinct red on the toilet paper and knew, a pit of excitement and sickness in my little belly.

I called my mom into the bathroom to request help and a pad, and she tearfully congratulated me. She then went into my brother's room where my brothers, age 11 and 15, were playing a video game. She announced, "Your sister is a WOMAN!" and they replied, "Ew." More embarrassment.

A few weeks later, my friend invited me over to swim in her pool and I had to ask my mom how to put in a tampon. I could NOT find my vagina but after a lot of effort and sweat, it was a painful success!

Through the years, cramps, ruined panties, missed opportunities for sex, and societal conditioning let me know my period was just straight-up nasty... something to dread. To hope it passes quickly, take some medicine, and go about my business.

In my mid-twenties, after bouts of amenorrhea from my eating disorders, my cramps started to become intensely painful, like labor pains. I was experiencing pretty intense pain one evening while working at the vintage shop in Tampa, Florida. My course of action was to ignore it, breathe through it, and maybe smoke enough weed on my break to numb it. My best friend and coworker happened to cut her thumb that evening and had to go to the ER. She looked at me and said, you're coming too. So I went, got a CAT scan, and two ovarian cysts were found. One had just burst and the other was the size of a plum. They sent me home with birth control to fix it and shrink the functional cyst and that was that.

A week later, I was in the same excruciating pain, trying to ignore it, dancing and drinking Jack and Gingers in a vintage bikini at a party. The next morning, I knew I couldn't ignore the pain any longer, and with a hangover, went back to the ER thinking it was another burst. Another CAT scan, and they discovered I had what is called a torsion, meaning the cyst shrank, dislodged, twisted my fallopian tube, and cut off blood supply to my ovary. I had to have emergency surgery to fix it. It was intense, painful, and moved me further from my womb and from myself.

A couple years later, deep into my healing journey and ready to reconnect with my period, I decided to try a menstrual cup and I've never looked back. In an effort to save on the expense of tampons and save Mama Earth, I learned to get up and personal with my vagina and my blood.

A few years in, I started to feel interested in tracking my cycle and really learning WTF is going on "down there".

Sister, what I've found is fascinating AF! Our cycles connect us to the power of Nature! When we are truly connected we even flow with the cycles of the moon! Beyond that, the different hormonal changes through our cycles can be HARNESSED. Our periods are actually magic, Goddess superpowers! We move through seasons, archetypes, and have a chance to harness different superpowers all within a moon cycle. It's

FASCINATING, and the more I learned, the more I healed my relationship with my womb.

Of course, in a Patriarchal world, anything cyclical rather than linear does not fit the mold. We have had to hide ourselves, cover the pain, and whistle along as though every day is the same and we can just operate like machines. When we deny our cycles (which DO NOT require a period or womb by the way) we hide our MAGIC. It's TRAGIC. Guess what, it is time to come out of hiding, to embrace the beauty of cyclical living. Of the moon. Of the seasons. Of birth and death and birth again. Life IS NOT linear and neither are our bodies. We spiral and wave like the goddamn sea that cannot be harnessed.

Recently, I learned that menstrual blood is high in stem cells (of course, it's meant to nourish an embryo) and makes an excellent face mask. Although slightly hesitant, on my moon, I decided to give it a go, painting my face like a damn warrior. It felt hot, it was full of *prana,* or life force energy, and it was magical! It ignited a fire within me and I cried at how long I have shunned this magic.

Ladies, our blood, our magic, our cycles are fucking powerful and it's time to come out of hiding. Put on our moon mask like warpaint! We ride at dawn, Queens!

Moon Cycle Magic

Phase 1: Menstrual Phase

Moon Phase: Often associated with the New Moon

Hormonal Happenings: Hormones are at a lull across the board.

Superpowers: We are intuitive, reflective, and decisive.

Season: Winter, we slow down.

Female Archetype: The Crone

Phase 2: Follicular Phase

Moon Phase: Often associated with the First Quarter Moon

Hormonal Happenings: Uptick in estrogen and serotonin. We feel happy and energized.

Superpowers: We are creative, playful, and able to initiate projects, plans, and ideas. This is a great time for manifestation work.

Season: Spring. Everything is in bloom.

Female Archetype: The Maiden

Phase 3: Ovulation

Moon Phase: Often associated with the Full Moon

Hormonal Happenings: A major upsurge in estrogen.

Superpowers: We are magnetic, alluring, sensual, and energized. This is a great time to socialize and put ourselves out there.

Season: Summer, baby!

Female Archetype: The Mother

Phase 4: Luteal Phase

Moon Phase: Often associated with the Last Quarter Moon

Hormonal Happenings: Estrogen levels descend as we prepare to bleed. Our energy slows and turns inward.

Superpowers: We wind down projects, have a keen editing eye, and start to slow down. We set boundaries and prepare to menstruate.

Season: Autumn. This is a time of transition and harvest.

Female Archetype: The Wild Woman

Reflection:

Whether you bleed or not, do you feel and track your body's cycles? How can you embrace your cycles more? Do you allow yourself to rest when your body needs it?

Embodiment Practice:

Where are you in your cycle today? If you bleed, you can use the Moon Cycle Magic chart above to pinpoint your cycle phase. If not, you can use the chart to find the associated moon phase. Look at your superpower and choose an activity to celebrate your power today!

Example:
Phase 1: A warm bath and meditation
Phase 2: Plan a project and take time to play
Phase 3: Get together with friends or go on a date
Phase 4: Wrap up a project

Day 11: I Own My Sexuality

When I was a little girl, I was extremely curious about sex. No one around me talked about it, but I wondered what my parents were doing when they locked their door. I saw people kissing on television and my parents would ask me to cover my eyes. But damn, did I want to peek. I was allowed to put posters of the New Kids on the Block, Jonathan Taylor Thomas, and Fred Savage on my walls, torn from *Tiger Beat* magazine. I didn't know why they made me feel a certain way, but I enjoyed imagining they were my boyfriends. Once on an episode of *Wonder Years*, Fred Savage, or little Kevin, tried a cigarette. I was so hurt and upset that I tore his picture off of the wall. He was out of the boyfriend club. I would secretly make my girl Barbies kiss and go under the covers, although I didn't know what happened beyond the kissing. I just knew it felt good and secretive and naughty. I would climb the soccer goal during my brother's practices, loving the tingly feeling it gave me but not daring to ask about it. I would watch *The Little Mermaid* and hope and pray that I would look like her someday, and that I too would find a prince, or maybe a gorgeous mermaid to kiss me and validate my worthiness. My neighbor, a couple years older than me, would corner me in the backyard when no one was watching and make us both take off our pants and touch our bums together. I didn't know why, but I knew I should probably keep that a secret.

One day, when I was 7, I overheard my mother explaining what sex is to my 9-year-old brother. Being super nosy, I held my ear to his door, but couldn't quite make out the details. I then begged my mother to tell me and she graciously laid out the practical details. I thought it was completely disgusting and knew that it was definitely only something married people do to be closer and to make babies.

At 13, I had my first kiss from a boy, short and fleeting, but in general had very little attention from boys, although I was desperate for it. The Disney programming had set in and I knew that I needed a handsome Prince to love me in order to be whole. The same year, my dad took me to buy a beautiful gold and emerald ring, a promise that I would save my virginity for marriage.

At 16, ready to rebel, knowing my friends had had sex, and just wanting it to not be a big deal, I lost my virginity to my boyfriend who was definitely homosexual. Everyone but me knew it, including him. I think he wanted to prove to himself and his super-conservative parents that he wasn't gay, and I wanted to get closer to him and run through the gates of adulthood. Needless to say, after a few drinks for courage, neither of us were that into it, and the sex was terrible.

In the next several years, I developed a dysfunctional relationship with sex and men. I carried both an overwhelming desire for sex and connection along with a pervasive sense of shame and secrecy. I wore my father's promise ring with ambivalence and deep fear of him finding out I had broken the promise. Also, since I was sure sex was connected with love and commitment, I thought that if I gave myself to someone, they would love me. I used it for validation and the strong desire to feel completed by someone, and the boys and men used me, well, for the pussy. I thought I was adult and empowered, but I was actually a hurt little girl in a woman's body.

In adulthood, after years of disappointment, feeling unlovable, and being taken advantage of, I was very disconnected from my body and slept around without connecting to my emotions or the other person. I didn't realize what had happened, put up a strong guard, and became very unconscious about sex. Finally, sick of my own shit and of not taking ownership of my sexual power, I decided to take a long hiatus to just worry about myself, hang out with my girlfriends, and explore self-pleasure practices. This pause was exactly what I needed to take my power back.

About a year into my hiatus I met my now husband. He had a lot of boundaries around sex and a lot more experience than me due to being older. We waited quite some time to consummate the relationship, but in the meantime, I was never more attracted to anyone in my life. When the time finally came, I had never been treated with such care and attention by a partner. It created a level of safety for me to explore my wants and my pleasure, and for it to be seen and received without judgment.

Even through our marriage, I have overcome lingering shame and trauma around sex, and at times, haven't owned my power. But as I continue to embody my Inner Goddess, I forgive the little girl who thought a shining prince would make her whole. I embrace her curiosity, and her body and the attraction to bodies of all types of people, no matter their gender identity. I stand in my Inner Queen and claim my sexual sovereignty and queerness while also embracing and savoring a satisfying and spiritual monogamous hetero relationship.

Sister, we DESERVE to be turned on. We deserve to own our bodies and our pleasure. We deserve to explore sex without baggage and shame. We deserve to feel sexy as we are. We deserve for sex to just be sex and for it to be a gateway to the spiritual. We deserve to pleasure ourselves. We deserve to have a conscious partner or partners invested in our pleasure. We deserve to forgo sex when we want. We deserve to sleep with whomever we are attracted to, men, women, or gender non-conforming. We deserve for sex to be enthusiastically consensual. We deserve to treat ourselves as Queens and Goddesses. For the sacred feminine to arrive in forms of pleasure. We deserve the ecstasy of Source connecting with Source. We deserve the freedom to consciously and consensually fuck.

Reflection:
What is your relationship to sex? Is it a gateway to the divine or to satisfying your animal instinct? Do you make time to receive pleasure?

Embodiment Practice:
Draw the alphabet with your hips. Let your pelvis move fluidly and sensually as you create the ABCs, in capital, lowercase, and cursive letters. Then let your hips move how they'd like. How does it feel to let your Sacral sway and play?

Day 12: I Am a Creatrix

Your life is a work of art. And you're either consciously creating it or sticking to old unconscious patterns. Your work of art doesn't need to look like anyone else's, can use all of the colors and mediums you wish and can change course at any given moment.

Creativity, or the use of imagination, is available in abundance to every single one of us. Have you ever watched a three-year-old play? They are masters at harnessing creative power and creating whole worlds. It comes easily for them as they don't yet know the "rules" of life, have the time and space to explore, live in the moment, and do not carry attachment to whatever they are imagining.

As adults, this can be much more difficult to tap into. We lose the ease, become out of practice, and are constantly stuck in the past or future. We hold judgment, limiting beliefs, and self-consciousness. We have ideas about the productive use of time. We have a strong sense of how things "should be".

On top of that, is the pressure to make money from our creations. That creating for fun is a waste of time and that if we aren't good enough at something to make a side hustle of it, we should find something else to do.

Your creativity is not a commodity. It is an infinite current waiting to be noticed. Waiting to be invited in. Waiting to flow through your unique vessel to become a playful expression of the divine.

Creativity doesn't have to look like painting, writing, or playing music, although art is a beautiful medium for her. Creativity can be channeled in every moment if we're only brave enough to call her in. She lives in electric conversations, in taking a walk without agenda or destination, in lovemaking, in preparing a meal, in the way you move, dress, even breathe. She is an invitation to get out of your own way, step into the present moment and respond, not out of conditioning, but out of spontaneity and joy.

She lives in the plants, in the Sun, in the water, in the air. She is ecstatic, she is inspiration, she is joy. She is the solver of humanity's greatest problems and the catalyst for progress. In her whispers, we hear that absolutely anything is possible, if only we allow ourselves to imagine it first.

In the work of art that is your life, every experience you have becomes a medium of expression. Your traumas, your obstacles, your victories, your relationships, your thoughts, your actions, your emotions. Everything is blending and stroking and splashing your canvas. Everything is valuable and comes together to make a masterpiece.

And when you become conscious, awake, a co-creator of your manifestations, the work of art becomes even more masterful, more pleasing, more awe-inspiring. You see that you are not the only painter, but are in a dance of co-creation with the Goddess. That she flows through you, creating a masterpiece meant to inspire the world.

Sister, you deserve to break down your walls and create. When creativity whispers to you, let down your guard and dance with her. Don't worry about what others might think, if the creation is of value, or if it feels slightly uncomfortable at first. Your time, your medium, your self, is inherently valuable as you are a prism for all of the unique colors of the divine. You are both artist and muse, woman and Goddess, an embodied expression of the divine. As she shines through you, as you hold her in your womb, as you peel off the layers and dance, the vibration of the whole planet rises. Let the world see, feel, and know your creations. You are a damn work of art and you are so, so beautiful.

Reflection:

When do you feel most creative? Do you allow yourself to create without attachment to the outcome? How can you make space in your life for more creativity?

Embodiment Practice:

Write a haiku, or simple Japanese poem, about creativity. There are a few simple rules of a haiku:

1. There are three lines.
2. The first line has 5 syllables.
3. The second line has 7 syllables.
4. The third line has 5 syllables.
5. Punctuation is up to you.

Example:
Goddess sings through me,
Perfect vessel for her song.
Together we dance.

Day 13: I Embrace My Sisters

I invite you to the sacred sisterhood. A safe space for growth, expansion, accountability, celebration, vulnerability, and deep wells of bliss.

Many of us hold deep sister wounds, which can make embracing female friendships difficult. Misogyny can infiltrate the minds and hearts of women in our patriarchy, and instead of rising together, we push each other apart.

In the centuries of witch-hunting, women were encouraged to betray each other in order to keep themselves safe. *I am not a witch, SHE is a witch.*

In the centuries where women were men's property and could not easily hold titles or land, competing for men was about survival.

In modern times, the "cool girl" trope is a woman who eats and drinks like a man, shuns female friendships, but adheres to pleasing the male gaze.

And the competition starts early. When I was in preschool, there was a girl who could do a cartwheel, I couldn't and was horribly jealous. I remember laying in bed one night, visualizing this little girl cartwheeling and cartwheeling until cartwheeling her way straight off of a cliff, Wile E. Coyote style. In my admiration of her physical prowess, I could have asked her to teach me, but instead, I was a 3-foot red-headed hater. How had I already picked up our cultural messaging that there is a scarcity of greatness for women?

In middle school, my best friend started getting pretty close to the popular crowd, literally. Every morning before first hour, the kids would all filter into the gymnasium while busses dropped us off to school. The popular kids would sit and form a circle, flirting, being precocious, chatting about crushes and make-outs. Then there were the rings of kids around them, each outward ring descending in social order, desperate to get in the center. One day, my best friend finally was invited into the center circle. I was just behind her and I remember her purposely turning her back to me as if to say, goodbye forever, I have reached ascension and you have no place with me anymore. Ouch.

Sister, I have a secret. This competition, this internalized misogyny, this idea that we have to tear others down to lift ourselves up, is a big fat lie designed to keep the sisterhood weak. To keep us from forming a mega-village of bodacious babes who rise up and take over. The mean girls, the mom-shamers, the body-shamers, the real housewives, the literal competition gameshows where the prize is a big dumb hunk, the social media shaming, the workplace drama, the gossiping, and the backstabbing is keeping each of us from truly stepping into our own power and rising together. This is the patriarchy, the wounded feminine.

There is an antidote. By doing the self-work to live without shame, to stand in your power, to see through illusion, to stand in your sovereignty and your truth, and to embody your Inner Goddess, will free you from the prison of internalized misogyny. By you fully being YOU out loud and on purpose, your inner flame will rise. And that flame is eternal, baby. It is NOT meant to be hoarded, but shared. You can use it to light up your sisters, to help them stand in their own power. To celebrate them, to let them know how proud you are of them, of US! You can inspire them to see their own beauty, their own strength, their own purpose. The cool girl knows her own power and uses it to lift her sisters up. The Goddess lives in all of us and it's time for her to COME OUT!

Be aware, there WILL be those who are triggered by your ENOUGHNESS. The haters, the shamers, the dream-dashers and naysayers. You are shining a light on their wounds and they do not yet possess the bravery to step into their own wholeness.

And that's OK. We cannot make anyone wake up to their own wholeness, but we can be shining examples of vulnerability and strength.

And in the process of becoming radically whole, know that there are others who might trigger YOU along the way. Notice when this happens, without judging or shaming yourself. Let yourself breathe into the sensation this brings up in your body, and ask this pain what it is trying to communicate with you. Maybe she's outwardly sexual and your pain is telling you that you are repressing your divine sexuality. Maybe she is outspoken and articulate and your pain is telling you that you are afraid to use your voice. Maybe she is living in abundance and your pain is telling you that you are non-deserving of such luxury. Let yourself FEEL your triggers. Treat them as sacred. Thank them for being helpful guideposts for your embodiment journey.

Sisters, we weren't meant to do this alone. When we come together vulnerably, when we sing, we dance, we share, we cry, we create, we hold each other, we rage together, we meditate together, and we RISE together. And when we rise together, the whole world feels it. Our collective voices of gentle power will crumble old structures and make way for a more balanced, feminine, and blissful existence.

Embrace your sisters, heal your wounds, and watch the magic unfold.

Reflection:

What triggers you about other women? What sensation does this cause in your body? What might this pain be trying to tell you?

Embodiment Practice:

Reach out to one of your girlfriends and shower her with love. Let her know why you are grateful for her, what her strengths are, and how much you love her.

Day 14: I Receive Fully

Sister, do you allow yourself to fully receive?

Many of us are nurturers, either by nature or by societal conditioning. Especially us spiritual queens, we want to help, to serve, to care for the ones we love. And that is a beautiful thing. But do you ever use service as a way to deflect being truly seen? Is it just easier being in the position of service?

Ladies, we were made to receive. Our wombs (physical and energetic) are cauldrons. They are a space to hold our magic, intentions, and manifestations. Our yonis (or vaginas) were made to receive pleasure, love, and magic. The more we disconnect from these spaces in our bodies, or use them unconsciously, the more we block ourselves from truly receiving the abundance and magic in this world.

The wounded feminine believes she doesn't deserve to receive, that her only value is in service and giving. Perhaps her womb and yoni have been the recipients of disrespect or abuse, of cultural conditioning, of birth trauma, ancestral trauma. Maybe we learned that it's safer to give because it gives us more control. Maybe we've been told receiving is selfish because there are many people and industries that benefit from us over-giving and being boundary-less.

Goddess, please give yourself permission to fully receive the abundance of the world around you. Your Sacral Chakra is begging to be released from this blockage, and to let the flow of energy, the dance between giving and receiving, the currency of *prana* to flow, flow, flow.

When someone gives you a compliment, instead of deflecting, say thank you and mean it. Let it fill every fiber of your being with appreciation and joy. When someone gives you a gift, receive it with pleasure and without the immediate energetic obligation to return the favor. When you're eating a delicious meal, allow yourself to truly TASTE it. To feel it in your body and to appreciate all of the hands that touched the food, from farmer to chef. When you are in nature, allow yourself to truly be with Mama Earth, to appreciate her beauty, to soak in her gifts. When you hear a good song, let your body feel the music and let the sound dance in your ears with pleasure. When you've accomplished something, let yourself slow down and celebrate rather than critiquing it or moving right along to the next thing. Allow yourself to use your good skin care, to light your good candles, to linger in the bath, to rest, to receive physical affection, to roll in the ecstasy of life.

Sister, by blocking receiving, you are taking away someone's right to give. When giving from a true place of love and service, doesn't it feel amazing? Don't you love seeing someone open a gift you spent extra time choosing? Don't you love seeing the pleasure of your partner when you're making love? Don't you love being someone's shoulder to cry on? Let others do the same for you!

And if you're giving when you're burnt out, the energetic current ceases to flow. It gets stuck inside your being and turns sour. We become martyrs, we become bitter, we become exhausted. The giving is no longer potent, it comes with too much baggage.

A few years ago, in a woman's retreat, I was in circle with my sisters. Each was taking a turn in the center of the circle while the other sisters shined love upon them with all their energy. I loved giving all of this love to each woman, but when my turn came, I immediately wanted to run. I didn't want to be seen, I didn't want to receive. I cried and cried, and the more I cried, the more I softened. My tears felt as though they flowed from my womb, and the more I released, the more I received. It was a beautiful breakthrough moment.

Tears can be a beautiful gateway to the sacred feminine. The more we release stuck energy inside us through tears, dancing, vocalizing, journaling, and other embodiment practices, the more we let go. The more we surrender to her flow. The more gifts we are able to receive. The more we soften. The more we relax. The more we find joy. The more we align ourselves with what we truly need and want. The more we embody our Inner Goddess. The more we receive.

And damnit, Queen, we deserve it!

Reflection:
Do you find it easier to give or receive? What do you enjoy about giving? What might be keeping you from truly receiving?

Embodiment Practice:
It's time to get brave and vulnerable and ask a sister or loved one to tell you what they love about you. When they tell you, try not to mentally refute anything they are saying. Instead, receive the words with gratitude and acceptance.

Week Three

The Solar Plexus Chakra

We continue this week with our energetic powerhouse, the Solar Plexus Chakra, or *Manipura*. Located just above the navel, this chakra governs our inner fire, our purpose, self-worth, and self-trust. Embodying the Inner Goddess by balancing the Solar Plexus invites us to take up space, claim our worth, move with purpose, and harness our inner warrior. We will move this world boldly, brightly, and unapologetically as we stand up for what is right and demand positive and impactful change.

I invite you to take a moment and place your hands on your upper abdomen. Take several deep breaths and focus your energy and attention on the Solar Plexus Chakra. See it spinning, a ten-petaled flower burning bright yellow as the Sun. Imagine it's like a pilot light. You can turn it up when you need to expend big energy and turn it down when you need rest, but it never burns out. Feel it whirling with power, purpose, confidence, and forward motion. You might fill the chakra with its sacred sound, *Ram*, by chanting it deeply three times. Then release with a breath in through the nose, and out through the mouth.

Within this current paradigm and suppression of the sacred feminine, many of us suffer from feeling not-enough. We put others' needs before our own. We put other people on a pedestal. We are our own harshest critics. We feel weak. We have forgotten our soul's purpose. And we are hungry for change. This week, as you mine through these feelings, I encourage you to be your own biggest cheerleader. To "try on" confidence and see how it feels. And to be gentle on yourself when you witness yourself slip. I also encourage you to take a moment and celebrate the tremendous amount of work you have put into your development, joy, and realization of your wholeness so far. You're such a badass and I'm proud of you!

Solar Plexus Chakra (*Manipura*)
Location: Just above the navel
Energy: Self-trust, Confidence, Purpose
Color: Yellow
Sacred Sound: Ram
Element: Fire
Overactive Chakra Symptoms: Overinflated ego. Perfectionism. Short temper.
Underactive Chakra Symptoms: Powerlessness. Low Self-Esteem. Lack of purpose.
When in Balance: We are confident and self-assured. We have purpose and a strong sense of self. We feel above or below no one.

Connect to the Solar Plexus Chakra with:
Food: Peppers, Protein, Bananas, Pineapple
Scents: Lemon, Peppermint, Fennel
Crystals: Citrine, Pyrite, Yellow Topaz
Activities: Goal-setting, Strength Training, any bold action

Day 15: I Am Enough

I invite you to look into the mirror and say to yourself, "I am enough." For real, take a moment and try it... I'll wait.

OK, now how did that feel? Silly? Empowering? Terrifying? Where did you feel it in your body?

I've found for most women, we are totally certain we are not enough. Between societal and cultural expectations, our Inner Child's wounds, and shame from our failures, our egos have become bruised. My dad used to quote the Bible to me saying, "to whom much is given, much is expected," and while it's true, I always had the feeling that I wasn't deserving, could never give enough to earn my privilege, and could never ever be enough.

I remember when I was studying for my first yoga certification, my yoga teacher, Jennifer Yarro, was lecturing on the energy body and ego. That an overinflated sense of ego is a sign of Solar Plexus imbalance, and how as yoga teachers, we need to keep it in balance to hold reverence for the practice and to keep our roles as humble guides in mind. I raised my hand and asked, "What if our problem is we never feel good enough? That we're hard on ourselves? That we are imposters?"

She answered that that is also ego. Not enough-ness is also an imbalance because the soul is always enough. I never thought of myself as egotistical until that day and it has helped me so much when those feelings arise to remember who I truly am. That I can stand in my power and confidence while also holding humility. Because I am spirit embodied and so is EVERYONE if only we remember. I have had the honor to pass on this teaching to my students.

One of my favorite workshops I've led to date, given to me from my teachers, is called "Awakening Your Inner Goddess". It involves a practice where we embody different goddesses with yoga, music, chanting, and rest. We first journey through Parvati, the mother. Then Durga, the warrior. Kali, the destroyer. Saraswati, goddess of the arts, and Lakshmi, goddess of abundance.

The first time I led this was to my first cohort of yoga teacher trainees in 2018, a powerful group of 30 women. From students, to professionals, to florists, police officers, and military, the energy of this group was powerful and impressive.

As we moved into the energy of warrior Durga, Beyoncé blaring, the students were invited to hold Warrior II pose and repeat after me: "I am STRONG! I am POWERFUL! I am BEAUTIFUL! I AM ENOUGH!" As they held the powerful posture, I encouraged them to repeat these mantras over and over, intensity and volume increasing. As I looked around the room at these 30 powerhouses, I saw tears streaming down their faces, a well of pain being transmuted into power.

I could feel the tears pouring down my own face, the anger being released, the rising of the sacred feminine embodied and visceral.

Sister, listen closely. You are not too much. You are not too little. You are enough. It doesn't matter what your career is, what grades you got in school, how much money you have, how intelligent you are, how sexy you feel, how big or small your body is, what you've accomplished today, whether or not you have a partner or children, where you live, or how many Instagram followers you have. Forget what society says. Rewrite your thoughts. Screw all messaging that says otherwise. You are enough. You are more than enough. You are Goddess incarnate and you are EVERYTHING, Queen!

Reflection:

Do you ever feel "not enough" or "too much"? Where did you receive these messages? What would it feel like to know you are equal to all other humans?

Embodiment Practice:

I invite you to find the yoga asana, Warrior II. Standing, spread your arms out to your sides and widen your feet to the width of your wingspan. Point your right toes to the right and your left toes straight forward, aligning your right heel with your left arch. Bend your right knee so it is directly over your right heel and gaze over your right fingertips. Repeat the mantra, "I am strong, I am powerful. I am beautiful. I am enough," three times and with feeling. Repeat on the other side.

Day 16: I Am Not Sorry

Early in my marriage, my husband said to me, "Have you noticed that you say 'I'm sorry' a lot?"

My response: "Oh my god, I'm so sorry!"

Facepalm.

I don't know when I started feeling the need to constantly apologize for my actions, my words, my mere existence. But he was right. I said it all the freaking time. Like a not-so-sacred mantra, or punctuation at the end of my sentence.

I was a master apologizer. Did someone else wrong you? I'm so sorry! Did you bump your knee on the couch? I'm so sorry! Did I not respond to your text within 5 minutes? I'm so sorry! Were you in my way when I was walking down the grocery aisle? I'm so sorry!

When you say it that often, does it even have meaning?

Yes, but it's not the intended one. It's not, "I sympathize with you," or "Wow, I really wish that wouldn't have happened." It's, "Maybe if I say this enough, you'll excuse me for my pitiful existence. I am powerless. I'd like to shrink myself to nothing. Your joy, comfort, and safety are a priority over mine. Please, walk all over me!"

Ouch.

After he so lovingly pointed this out to me, I noticed just how often this came out of my mouth, like a nervous tic or a sneeze. And I felt devastated.

The truth is, I felt sorry for myself. For not understanding myself. For not feeling purposeful. For all of my failures. For not being enough or doing enough. Maybe, just maybe, I would get the love I wanted if I just apologized and conceded to the subordination of sorry. My trauma response was always to fawn and the sorry was the exchange rate for people-pleasing and avoiding confrontation.

But when he gave me permission to stop apologizing, I was able to shine the light of awareness on this behavior. I would notice when I wanted to say it, pause, and then ask myself, "Am I REALLY sorry?"

And that awareness, that pause, that questioning gave me the opportunity to start rewriting my story. To start believing that not everything was my fault. To imagine the possibility that I wasn't less than. That what other people thought of me wasn't actually my concern. That I'm not fucking sorry, I'm just fucking human.

Sister, allow me to invite you to do the same. To stop yourself in your tracks when "I'm sorry" is about to escape your beautiful mouth, and instead say nothing. Or say what you REALLY mean.

We don't have to be sorry for being outside of the mold of societal standards. We don't have to be sorry for our feminine bodies. We don't have to be sorry for our opinions, our beliefs, our preferences, or our identities. We don't have to be sorry for our existence. In fact, we are allowed to have unabashed pride in all our weird, wild wonderfulness. For the space we get to take up. For the longings of our souls, our wisdom, our intelligence.

Don't get me wrong, sometimes an apology is due. If we are in the wrong, we put on our big girl pants and own the shit out of it. But if we're not, let it go, sister!

I am here. I am NOT sorry. I own my sovereignty, my worth, my unique expression and, Goddess, you should too. Free yourself from the tyranny of sorry and be yourself unapologetically! You are the Goddess incarnate and she only stands in the power of the divine, above and below no one, unabashedly here.

No, I'm not fucking sorry. I'm a fucking Goddess.

Reflection:
Do you find yourself apologizing often? If so, is this done consciously or unconsciously? What are alternatives to saying, "I'm sorry"?

Embodiment Practice:
Set aside a few minutes for mantra meditation inspired by the late Buddhist monk, Thich Nhat Hanh. Find a comfortable seat, allowing your spine to lengthen and your shoulders to soften. Close your eyes or soften your gaze downward. Take a few moments to tune into your breath, lengthening your inhales and exhales. After a few deep breaths, inhale and say to yourself silently, "Inhale, I take up space." Then exhale and say, "Exhale, I am worthy." Repeat for several minutes, not only saying the words, but inviting in and embodying the feeling of worthiness. When you're complete, notice how you feel.

Day 17: I Am Strong AF

For a long time, I did not consider myself as strong. In my early childhood, things tended to flow easily for me and I was able to accomplish things through joy and following my natural instinct. Strength takes resistance, and in my childhood world of confidence and energy, there was not much to push against.

As I got older and started meeting resistance, I felt very weak. I was overcome with anxiety and depression. I starved myself into fragility. My emotions made me feel helpless. My inability to thrive within a prescribed societal mold made me feel less-than. Multiple educational failures, failed relationships, and lack of true direction weighed me down and created resistance which I found impossible to push against.

I started a regular and intentional yoga practice at a time where I was willing to try anything to feel better, to break out of my inner prison. At first I felt out of touch with my body, several years removed from my elite dance training. Although the yoga felt good, which kept me coming to class, balancing was really hard, my body felt rigid, and my mind had to work really hard to focus.

But the more I showed up, the more strength I built. The more confidence I had. The more my muscles remembered how they used to stretch and balance and leap. My body went from frail to muscular, my mind became stronger, and I felt the possibilities of my life opening up. I remember the ecstasy of balancing in Crow pose for the first time. After weeks of trying, bruises on my arms, I placed my hands on the mat, balanced my knees onto my upper arms, and suddenly my feet lifted off the mat. Incredible! For the first time in a long time, I wasn't moving my body to achieve an aesthetic result, but to increase my confidence and mental fortitude.

A few years later, I was feeling a bit stuck again. I was running my yoga studio, building my business, and feeling burnt out. My muscles weren't supporting my joints in my yoga practice and I started feeling some pain. I decided to hire a personal trainer and learn how to strength train.

Even with my dance and yoga background, I never considered myself an athlete. My parents enrolled me in soccer at age 4 and I just remember sitting at the goal drawing pictures in the dirt and hoping and praying for halftime so I could chat with the other kids and eat a snack. With my athletic career starting and ending at age 4, I never felt very comfortable in a gym and had to stretch myself mentally to start this journey of lifting heavy things surrounded by a bunch of men.

I hired the nicest trainer I could find (thanks, Hannah!) and we began my journey of building physical strength. After the first session, I could barely walk down the stairs I was so sore. But little by little, I was able to lift more and more, and recover more quickly. I started to feel at home in the gym and built even more confidence in my body's capabilities.

Through my pregnancy and the pandemic, I continued to strength train. In fact, I was still doing semi-heavy deadlifts the day I went into labor! My devotion to both my strength training and yoga practices allowed me to endure the day-to-day chaos of the world with relative grace and trust in myself to keep going.

After Gemma was born, I realized I was unconsciously mentally preparing for the utter marathon that is motherhood. Everyday requires a level of endurance that I never thought I was capable of. It doesn't matter how I am feeling, I show up for my daughter because I am endlessly devoted to her. Because she is worth it. I show up when I'm tired, when I am sick, when I am grieving, when I am scared. I show up. And I am so very proud of that.

Inner strength requires devotion to something larger than you and the practice of overcoming resistance over and over. For me, the devotion to myself now that I know I am absolutely worth it, the devotion to my daughter, the devotion to those I serve, and the devotion to the sacred feminine are what motivate me to show up for my life every day. The challenges will come, but I now have the confidence and muscle to meet them with grace.

Goddess, you, your life, your purpose are worth fighting for. By stepping up to life's challenges, you are creating fertile soil to blossom and grow. As these challenges integrate into your being, your story becomes your strength. You are worth it. The world needs you. And even if you don't know it yet, you are strong AF.

Reflection:
What resistance have you overcome to gain strength in your life? What makes you feel weak? What makes you feel strong?

Embodiment Practice:
I invite you to a 5-day plank challenge. For plank pose, you may have either your hands or forearms on the ground, legs extended behind you balancing on either your toes or knees. Align your head, shoulders, hips, and knees into a straight line. Gaze slightly forward, press the Earth away with your hands/forearms, and draw your navel toward your spine.

Day 1: Hold for 10 seconds
Day 2: Hold for 20 seconds
Day 3: Hold for 30 seconds
Day 4: Hold for 45 seconds
Day 5: Hold for 1 minute

Day 18: I Trust My Gut

Do you trust your gut?

While your intuition comes from your highest self, the gut connects you to the instincts of the animal self. Our bodies provide us with so much valuable information at any given moment and it takes a lot in a disconnected society to be able to tune into the body's cues, let alone trust its knowledge.

When I lived in Chicago in my early 20s, I enrolled in college to study fashion design. Although I had never sewed before, I thought my innate creativity and artistic eye would make fashion a good career choice. After dropping out of my first university, losing my scholarship, and moving to Chicago with a boy against my parents' wishes, I felt lost and bruised. This felt like an opportunity where I could prove myself and my worth. Did it seem like my soul's purpose to design and make clothing? No, but it seemed good enough, the school accepted me, and my parents approved of this new direction.

When I first started school, the tuition cost and materials cost were numbers so high I didn't even understand, but the enrollment advisor assured me that I would find a career that easily paid off my student loans. Knowing it was a big investment, I dove into the materials and became a star student. I easily passed all of my general education courses with flying colors and my drawing skills quickly improved. I received a lot of praise from my teachers and enjoyed the other students.

But there was one problem. I absolutely hated sewing. I didn't mind making patterns, choosing fabrics, cutting them out, but I absolutely hated the sewing machine. It was a skill that, no matter how hard I tried, just eluded me. I, of course, was in total denial of this truth. I kept pushing along, kept purchasing all of the expensive art school materials, kept trying to fit into the identity of a fashion designer.

I think I was probably two semesters in when I knew in my gut this wasn't the career for me. I enjoyed certain classes and I liked the security of "knowing" my future career, but my soul wasn't happy. I would get off the train and walk to school, cumbersome supplies in hand, and tell myself that I only have to commit to this for the next couple of decades until the loans are paid off.

Soon enough, my body started revolting. I would grab all of my supplies, take a bus to my train, and take the train into the city. All the while, my belly would ache. It would get worse and worse while my body filled with anxiety. One day, I got off the train and instead of taking my usual route to school, I immediately boarded the next train home. I skipped class, and while the ache in my belly eased immediately, it got worse as the days went by and I realized that I had fallen behind.

I wish I could say that I realized I needed to choose myself and walk away then, but this cycle went on much longer. The more I skipped, the more anxiety I had, the sicker I felt. I failed the class and felt devastated and disappointed in myself. Plus, I was burdening my future self with all of the loan money wasted.

At the same time, I had a relationship I knew I needed to leave. I pinned that as the main problem, knowing that leaving the city and him would for sure be the change I needed. I found my school had another location in Tampa, Florida, broke up with my boyfriend, transferred, and that was that.

But of course, it wasn't. After a couple more semesters, at age 25, I finally dropped out. I was in mountains of student loan debt, felt I completely wasted several years of my life, my self-esteem was crushed, and I was certain I had no future. I had no degree, no clear life path, a psychological addiction to marijuana which I tried to use to self-treat my anxiety, and felt physically and emotionally crushed.

If I had initially listened to my gut, I could have avoided making so many choices that only served to hurt me. Over a decade later, I have a lot of compassion for younger Lauren (plus have a life that she couldn't have possibly imagined) but I still hold sadness that I was so intent on pleasing others and fitting into a mold that wasn't designed for me. I was unable to hear my body screaming, "This isn't right!"

Sister, are there parts of your life that don't feel aligned? When you tune into your gut, what is it telling you?

Queen, your gut is so intelligent, so wise. It knows what you need. Not what society or your parents want from you. Not what has worked for someone else. Your career, your relationships, your interests, your education, where you live, how you spend your time, whether or not you have children… that is no one's business but yours, and your gut is here to help you carve your own weird, wild, and wonderful trail of purpose.

Reflection:
Can you think of a time where you trusted your gut and it was right? Can you think of a time where you didn't trust your gut and should have?

Embodiment Practice:
Take a few moments to consider a decision you need to make, big or small. And consider two different outcomes. Place your hand on your Solar Plexus and close or soften your eyes. Think of the first outcome and notice your physical response, especially in the gut. Then consider the second outcome, also paying attention to your body's cues. Did your body give you helpful information?

Day 19: I Hold Sacred Anger

Sister, I've got something to tell you.

It's OK to be angry. It's your right to be very, very angry. You deserve to be very, very fucking angry.

Angry at war, angry at environmental destruction, patriarchy, colonialism, rape culture, white supremacy, control over women's bodies, at world leaders with far too much power, at the unfairness of loss and abandonment, being forced to have children, being forced to birth children while strapped down and on our backs, for slavery, for the pain of our ancestors, for the Earth our children are inheriting, for not being given a seat at the table, suppressing our voices, being put into boxes of virgin or slut, having to take on all of the burdens of the household, for industries designed to make us feel powerless so we'll buy shit, for governments who don't give a fuck about us, for being sold messages that our bodies are dirty, for being called witches or bitches, for them making us feel like our pussies aren't beautiful, for Instagram filters, having to be everything for everyone, for human trafficking, school shootings, the 24/7 news cycle, for all the dangerous chemicals in our products, for anyone claiming we are anything less than sovereign beings. FUCK ALL OF THAT.

Sister, have you been taught to swallow your anger? To be a good girl? To be the peacemaker? To be seen and not heard? FUCK ALL OF THAT TOO.

Sister, let me tell you something. Your rage is SACRED. Your RAGE will pierce through the BULLSHIT in this world. Your rage is a mother defending her child, a woman fighting back after her abuser has gone too far, a superhero defending Mother Earth, a Goddess defeating a demon. A woman, enduring millennia after millennia of dehumanization finally screaming ENOUGH!

For so long, I have been afraid of my anger. So afraid, that she became so repressed that she became my Inner Bully. My "you're not enough" or "you're too this". She became my eating disorder, my depression, my codependency, my smoking too much and drinking too much, my self-neglect, my self-harm. She was so determined to be seen that she attacked me from within until I couldn't take it anymore.

Sister, you do not deserve that shit! You deserve to call out the evil of patriarchy, domination, and destruction when you see it. You deserve to defend the children, the "freaks", and underprivileged of this world until your voice is hoarse. You deserve to scream, cry, and beat your fists to the Earth in sacred rage of its maltreatment. You deserve to speak your mind without fear of ridicule, shunning, or death.

Sister, our voices have been suppressed for so long because they are afraid of our POWER. They are afraid of our PEACE. They are afraid of our wombs and yonis with the power to give birth, pleasure, and connect to the secrets of this Earth. Those in power benefit from our suppression. Those in power want domination, control of resources, control of animals, control of humans, control of freaking outer space! They do not benefit from our messages of collaboration, of peace, of the knowledge that WE ARE ALL DIVINE and DO NOT need a middleman between us and Goddess. They do not benefit from us being educated, seeing things differently, of knowing our power to change the world.

Witches, use your voice. Harness your sacred rage. Let the old systems, old hierarchies, old shriveled balls crumble to the ground. It's time for a new paradigm.

But I warn you, sister, do not become lost in the rage or stuck in her. Let her rise, feel her, let her mobilize you into divine action, but claim your peace, let her pass, and embrace the feeling of the life and the world we are creating together. Move her from the fire of your belly to the ocean of the heart and allow her to live as sacred and righteous LOVE.

Let anger be the fire that bursts the heart wide open, that allows your hands to do Goddess's work, to build a world of equality, peace, connection, and *dharma*.

Sister, may you feel your anger completely, may you take sacred action, and may you Love with all of your being.

Goddess, you are so fucking powerful. It's time to rise.

Reflection:
Do you allow yourself to feel angry? Do you tend to internalize your anger or do you lash out at others? What stirs up anger in you? *Note, if this exercise at any point feels too overwhelming or triggering, give yourself permission to take breaks or come back to it later.

Embodiment Practice:
I invite you to explore Goddess Squats with Lion's Breath. Start with the feet wider than hip distance with toes pointed outward and heels inward. Inhale to reach the arms overhead and lengthen through the legs. Exhale to bring the arms to a cactus or goal-post shape (arms straight out to the side with elbows bent at 90 degrees) and bend the knees into a squat, making sure the knees align with the toes and stack over the heels. Continue to flow with the breath between these two shapes, adding Lion's Breath. For Lion's Breath, inhale through the nose. Then exhale out of the mouth, sticking out the tongue and perhaps crossing the eyes, allowing for a raspy roar. Repeat several times and notice how you feel.

Day 20: I Communicate My Boundaries

Sister, repeat after me. My boundaries are sacred. Now say it louder for the people in the back: MY BOUNDARIES ARE SACRED.

Women, myself included, hold societal, family, and ancestral expectations to do it all. To be a badass businesswoman, an amazing mother, a giving and sexually fulfilling partner, a housekeeper, a chef, a clown, a shoulder to cry on, and a goddamn super model. To be "enough" we have to be everything! And say yes to everything!

Sister, you cannot be everything for everyone all of the time. It's not only impossible, but it drains your life force, sets you up for resentment and disappointment, and teaches others not to respect you.

When you say yes to EVERYTHING, you are saying your *prana,* or your sacred life force energy, has little worth. That it's a cheap commodity free for the taking. Bitch, please, your *Prana* is worth EVERYTHING. Your time, and what you're able to experience within it, are sacred. Your worth is not based on how much value everyone gets from you but on how much you value your own time and energy. Your time and service are not an all-you-can-eat buffet. You are a gourmet 5 course meal and you're Michelin star, baby!

When you say yes to EVERYTHING, it's easy to slip into resentment. You're no longer serving or giving with an open heart, and instead, your heart closes and you're at an energetic deficit. The act of serving and of giving is so much more POTENT when it comes from a place of joy, abundance, and wholeness. Both the giver and receiver benefit so much more when your "yes" is a full body "hell yes" without doubt and uneven energy exchanges attached.

When you say yes to EVERYTHING, your value, in the eyes of the receiver, decreases. They know they can call on you for anything and everything so they do. And they know they don't have to give you an equal exchange of energy. They start to believe they are entitled to your time, resources, and energy. You become a slave to the "yes" and you're no slave, honey. You're a damn Queen.

When you say yes to EVERYTHING, you are saying no to yourself. You are denying your autonomy, your pleasure, your purpose, your worthiness.

And be honest with yourself, are you saying yes to everything because you are subconsciously denying yourself? Are you keeping so busy with the needs of others that you don't have to look in the mirror and claim who you are and what you want? Is it scary to own your pleasure, your sovereignty, your time? Is your self-worth dependent on others' approval and how much you're doing for them? It's time to reclaim your worth!

Baby, you are worthy. You deserve respect. You deserve pleasure. You deserve to know you're enough regardless of your output and regardless of others' opinions.

When you start saying no, and without excuses, you are standing in your own power. You are saying that you don't value others more than yourself. You are saying that you get to CHOOSE where your energy goes, and to flow in the direction of your own joy and destiny.

Boundaries provide a container in which your joy flows. You lay down your clear expectations for the pleasure of interacting with you, the exchange for your energy, your worth. It not only serves you, but the others in your life. Instead of half your energy, they get to receive all of you. Instead of resentment, they receive your open heart. Instead of a slave, they receive mutual respect. When the rules are set, you get to play the game. And the game can be really, really fun!

Goddess, it's time to claim your energy, give with an open heart, and to stand in your sovereignty. You are worth it, your time is worth it, your life is worth it!

R-E-S-P-E-C-T, that's what boundaries give to me, R-E-S-P-E-C-T, Inner Goddess, I embody! Wooooooo!

Reflection:
Do you every find yourself saying "yes" to things you ultimately regret and resent? Do you believe other people will not like you anymore if you start setting boundaries? What is one easy boundary you can set today for practice?

Embodiment Practice:
Take a few moments to imagine a golden bubble of light encompassing the space three feet around your body. Visualize yourself filling this space with compassion, honesty, and respect. Then visualize any negative or draining energy being blocked by the bubble. You can call on this bubble of protection anytime your energy or time feels violated and use it to embody the energy of respect and compassion as you lovingly communicate your needs and boundaries with others.

Day 21: I Am Bold

Sister, are you ready to boldly step into your life?

Yes, we can embody patience, slow transitions, and waiting to receive our manifestations. But sometimes you've got to put on your warrior goddess pants, boldly claim your desires, and make the big leap.

I'm talking about being straight-up gutsy. Do you feel nervous? Good. Because bravery doesn't happen in absence of fear but despite it.

To take bold action means to know what you want, gather your inner fire, and jump. It's accepting the consequences of your actions, knowing that while you may experience pushback, you'll also get to embody your most authentic badass self.

Sometimes it's hard to narrow down what we truly want. What society says, our parents say, what we've seen examples of, our old stories can all impede our ability to hear our Inner Goddess when she speaks. Maybe when you do hear her, you brush off her words as selfishness, or you feel like an imposter. Maybe it just seems like silly dreams that could never possibly manifest in the real world.

Sister, this is YOUR life. No one else gets to write the script but you. Your desires matter. Your needs matter. Your DREAMS matter. It's OK to be selfish sometimes. It's OK to want big things for yourself. It's OK to choose YOU. It's more than OK to step into your sacred soul path despite society or the people around you not understanding. Only YOU can hear your Inner Goddess and she is the only authority you need.

For YEARS I wanted to become a yoga teacher. It seemed impossible. I didn't know any yoga teachers. I couldn't afford to go to a yoga studio. My practice wasn't good enough. It wasn't the right time. But the desire, the whispers of my Inner Goddess were relentless.

One night, I couldn't sleep. It was one of those anxiety-ridden insomnia episodes where I was spiraling about every awful thing I've ever done and every person I've ever wronged. For instance, when I was 6, I was in the garden with my dad and 3-year-old brother. I had seen a cartoon character balance a broom in their hand so I figured it was totally possible, and extremely impressive, if I could balance a metal rake in one hand. Tada! Unfortunately, the rake crashed down onto my toddler brother's head, causing a bleeding gash. That kinda stuff.

Anyway, after enough time tossing and turning, I heard the quiet voice through all of the noise, telling me to become a yoga teacher. I got out of bed and onto my laptop. I started googling yoga teacher training. I found one that made my heart sing, and better yet, it was in Costa Rica! Fighting against my Inner Bully, but knowing in my gut this was the right choice, I took a deep breath, got out my debit card, and put down the deposit. One of the best decisions of my life and the catalyst for radical change and growth.

What is it that YOU truly want? It's time to let go of all the reasons not to follow your desires, gather the fire in your belly, take a deep breath, and LEAP!

Sign up for the course, book the trip, tell someone you love them, send the text, make the post, sing the song, initiate the breakup, ask for help, go to therapy, get a coach, cut your hair, wear the bikini, leave the job you hate, ask for the raise, set your boundaries, make the move, and shake it up!

Queen, consider this permission to BOLDLY step into the life of your dreams! There are so many reasons not to, but they do NOT trump the truth and power of your Inner Goddess.

Reflection:
What is something you deeply desire but have been too afraid to do? When you visualize yourself doing this thing, how do you feel? What is stopping you from it?

Embodiment Practice:
Do something that you desire that is out of your comfort zone. It can be big or small. I double dog dare you!

Week Four

The Heart Chakra

This week, we bridge the physical and ethereal realms with the Heart Chakra, or *Anahata*. Located in the center of the chest, aligned with the physical heart, this chakra is the energetic embodiment of Love. When it shines brightly, we know that we ARE Love. We freely give and receive love, we bear grace, and we feel a deep sense of bliss. When we disarm the Heart Chakra, we become compassionate keepers of the light. We have nothing to prove. And we feel intrinsically connected with the collective.

I invite you to take a moment and place your hands on your heart. Take several deep breaths and focus your energy and attention on the Heart Chakra. See it spinning, a twelve-petaled flower glorious and green. Imagine it holding all of the love from Earth and Spirit. A whirling vortex of compassion, gratitude, and connection. Its energy flows down to your lower chakras, and up to your higher ones, fortifying them with the power of love. You might fill the chakra with its sacred sound, *Vam*, by chanting it three times. Then release with a breath in through the nose, and out through the mouth.

I want you to see, feel, hear, and know the powerful magic of your heart. It is the altar in your body's temple. A perpetually flowering tree of life. As you consider your relationship with self-love, forgiveness, and joy, I invite you to witness the heart's beauty, even the beauty in its wounds and scars, with curiosity and compassion. You and your heart are worthy of healing, strengthening, and of changing the world for the better. By radical acts of love, you usher in the sacred feminine and let the old paradigm crumble. Let your heart dance, let your heart cry, and let your heart shine, Goddess!

Heart Chakra (*Anahata*)
Location: Center of the chest, the heart
Energy: Compassion, Love, Connection
Color: Green
Sacred Sound: Yam
Element: Air
Overactive Chakra Symptoms: Inauthentic relationships. Over-giving. Controlling.
Underactive Chakra Symptoms: Disconnection. Lack of Self-Love. Blocking Love from others.
When in Balance: We are able to freely give and receive love. We are empathetic toward ourselves and others. We allow others to be themselves. We are able to forgive.
Connect to the Heart Chakra with:
Food: Leafy Greens, Avocado, Dark Chocolate
Scents: Rose, Jasmine, Marjoram
Crystals: Green Fluorite, Rose Quartz, Pink Tourmaline
Activities: Breathwork, Yoga, Affirmation, Time with loved ones

Day 22: I Love Myself

It's a parent's job to love their child so fiercely that the child knows how to love themselves in the same way. Once the child has grown, in their independence, they can make decisions from a place of self-worth, confidence, and empowerment.

The problem is, most parents do not fully love themselves and have unresolved childhood trauma which gets passed onto their children. So it's a cycle. But we are here to break the cycle, and if we choose to have children, to do it from a place of self-love, consciousness, and healing.

I am so glad I waited to have my daughter until my mid-thirties, because before that, honey, I was a straight-up hot mess. I didn't understand myself, didn't fully love myself, and didn't know how to be in my body with ease.

I'm very lucky to have parents who always verbalized to me, and have shown me over the years, that they love me unconditionally. Unfortunately, being human and imperfect, they had unresolved issues that they inadvertently passed on to me and my siblings. They were young when they had us and were doing their best. However, I also know that they did such a wonderful job raising me, that I was in the position of privilege to even consider self-love as an essential part of life. Their parents, and their parents before them, were so entangled in just surviving that self-love was not available on the hierarchy of needs.

My father was quick to love and quick to anger. In a second, this large and jovial man would snap into a big scary monster to me. His nervous system was reactive and he had a fierce instinct to protect the family, which veered into overcontrol. He never physically abused us, but when he was angry, his words hurt and I always felt like I was walking on eggshells. I don't blame him. Being a man in the patriarchy is tough, and when they aren't allowed to be fully expressed in their sensitivity, creativity, and vulnerability, it often comes out in the worst of ways. I hid parts of myself from him, in deep desire of his approval, and to save him and myself from his potential outbursts.

As I grew into an adult, I knew it was safer to hide parts of me than to be fully authentic. I knew not EVERY part of me was worthy of love and I internalized knowing that if every part of me wasn't worthy, then **I** wasn't worthy.

My mother was EXTREMELY loving to all of her children, but was not loving toward herself, especially toward her beautiful body that grew, birthed, and nurtured us. Although she was always very positive about my body and extremely encouraging of my passions, her words toward herself cut me very deeply. I know that by turning this criticism inward, she was also breaking a generational cycle of body and beauty criticism. As women, looking presentable has been essential to our survival for as long as the patriarchy has existed. But, combined with the media, ancestral trauma, and my mother's lack of self-love, I internalized the messaging which was a contributing factor to many years of my disordered eating and self-loathing.

Many external factors form our repetitive thoughts and limiting beliefs. We aren't born disconnected from self-love, but we learn it from our families, peers, cultures, media, and religions. Like well-tread roads, over the years, these thoughts carve deep neural pathways, creating a tangled highway system of disfunction.

I am extremely grateful that I have been able to unwind and rewrite this mental and emotional programming through the years. When I was hospitalized for my eating disorder at age 17, thanks to my supportive and loving parents, I was introduced to the concept of positive affirmations. At the time, I found them so cringey. Looking at the mirror and saying to myself, "I am beautiful," or "I am worthy," felt so incredibly inauthentic. They were so far removed from my familiar pathways, and I was so uncomfortable with myself that I met the technique of affirmations with great skepticism.

It has not been a perfect, easy, or linear journey, but over time, and with a lot of practice, therapy, yoga, conversation with like-minded and loving souls, books like these, world travel, and other experiences that have revealed the true ME, I can absolutely affirm (without cringe) that I love myself. Affirmations are my friends and I welcome rewriting my mental story. It is my deepest prayer as a parent that I pass that love onto my daughter, and she is able to internalize and embody it unconditionally. No chains to break, no new programming needed. I know I am not "perfect" at least in the earthly sense, but hopefully it's enough.

When we get down to the bottom of things, to our highest and truest selves, to the realm of the Goddess, we ARE pure love. We are divine manifest. We are queens walking this Earth. And you can't mess with perfection. As the great and powerful Drag Queen superstar RuPaul says, "If you can't love yourself, how the HELL are you gonna love somebody else? Can I get an AMEN?"

Amen, Goddess. Amen.

Reflection:
Do you love yourself? What blocks you from self-love? List a few things you DO love about yourself.

Affirmation:
Look into the mirror and repeat to yourself the affirmation, "I am Loved. I am Loving. I am Love." It may feel foreign or uncomfortable at first, but try to embody the feeling of love. Let it fill you up. And when you gaze into your own eyes, know that love is looking back.

Day 23: I Center My Heart

Dear one, your heart is the sacred bridge between the Earth and the divine.

With her central placement, she combines the rooted experiences of your lower chakras with the ethereal mysteries of the higher chakras.

She is the shimmering portal between worlds, the place where we hold the truth of our bodies and souls.

She is the altar of our body temple, a sacred place of ritual and worship.

Sister, in a world where most people make decisions from the head, I urge you to listen to the longings of the heart. She is intelligent, she is divine, and most importantly, she longs to travel in the direction of your highest joy.

When she is open and centered, she beams like a Care Bear Stare, illuminating the world. When she is closed, her light can be eclipsed by the world.

Her state can manifest physically in the body. One important skill that my yoga teacher passed onto me is body reading. We can observe your posture, stance, and gait to learn your body's story. One hip might be higher than the other because you've spent so much time resting your child there. Or perhaps your feet point outward from years of dance training.

When I look at most people, from children to elders, I see the shoulders slumped forward with an exaggerated convex curve in the upper back. From a young age, we sit in chairs. We slump over our books, computers, phones, and steering wheels. The muscles of the upper back become long and weak. The muscles of the chest become short, tight, and weak. For those in female bodies, this might be extra pronounced because of the weight of the breasts and the unconscious desire to hide them.

This body patterning comes from an emotional place as well. When I have been in the peaks of disordered eating and depression, the elegant posture of ballet training would slowly fade. I'd start to curl into myself, protecting my broken heart, hiding my shame. This is what I see en masse from our adaptation to technology and disconnection from each other.

Sister, we are in a world where our hearts are eclipsed. We are in the dark. But you, your Inner Goddess embodied, are a lighthouse. Your sisters, embodying their Inner Goddesses, even more light. We bravely open our hearts and follow the direction of our joy, and together, we are stars that light up a galaxy.

When my daughter was born, I felt my heart burst wide open. I felt an exponential increase in love that came with a deep sense of fear, a need to protect this precious being. While the fear hasn't left me completely, I've become accustomed to this heart-open state, more attuned to its joy and power.

Can it feel vulnerable and scary to open the heart? Yes. If you've been working at a desk for 15 years, your first backbend in yoga might feel very uncomfortable. But over time, the chest opens, the back strengthens, your heart is shining forth and your body fills with effervescence. So too is the practice of energetically opening the heart.

So tend to your inner altar. Your bridge between worlds. Breathe into her and allow her to slowly blossom. Let the world feel your joy, be bathed in compassion, and the warmth from your light.

Sister, let's do it together. For ourselves. For humanity. Pinky promise?

Reflection:

Do you tend to guard your heart? What does it mean to you to "open your heart"? What does it feel like in your body?

Embodiment Practice:

Roll up a blanket or towel into a long skinny shape, 3-4 inches in diameter. Lay down on your back, placing the towel-roll just under the tips of your shoulder blades, perpendicular to the length of your body. Allow the arms to relax in a cactus shape, or 90 degree angle. Encourage the whole body to soften as you breathe deeply for 5 minutes, allowing the chest to open. For extra potency, add the mantra, "Inhale, my heart opens. Exhale, I invite joy into my heart."

Day 24: I Forgive

Sister, you do not have to live your life perfectly. Never harming a soul, never putting your foot in your mouth, never making a mistake.

Earth is a school, and a big part of learning and growing is failing. We stumble as we grow, and sometimes our stumbles can have collateral damage.

It's inevitable that as we rack up the years on this plane, we also accumulate a number of regrets. That even if we live a wholesome life which we are extremely proud of in this present moment, there can still be memories that pop in to say hello every once in a while that stab our hearts with pain and shame.

We can ask others for forgiveness, hoping it absolves the pain in our hearts, and while it might help us heal and move on, it is only part of what unlocks us from the prison of shame.

You see, forgiveness is for the forgiver, not the forgiven. It allows the forgiver to release the resentment and the anger weighing their hearts down.

Sister, to release yourself from shame, you must shine the light of compassion on your own heart. When you feel into a moment that brings you shame, ask these questions:

Is it possible that you were doing the best you could at the time?
Is it possible that you were responding from trauma?
Is it possible that it actually changed the direction of your life for the better?
Is it possible that you learned and grew from the situation?
Is it possible that you are human and that being human means making mistakes?

Sister, free yourself from resentment, from shame, from stagnant self-anger. Give yourself permission to let go.

Forgive your Inner Child. Forgive your Inner Teenager. Your Inner Adult. Commune with your Inner Goddess and ask her to bathe all versions of you in compassion and peace.

Holding onto the hurt is like tying bricks to your feet and trying to swim.

Sister, let go. Let yourself float in the waters of the goddess. Let her waters of forgiveness move you into the direction of freedom, of purpose, of radical love.

Look back at the former versions of you like a benevolent mother. You are a child of the goddess and Goddess herself. As you play, as you grow, as you move through this Earth school, give yourself permission to stumble. Know that each "failure", each act of self-betrayal, when composted with compassion and watered with the tears of forgiveness, becomes the fertile soil for the garden that is your life.

Queen, it's time to forgive yourself. To breathe into your heart with compassion. To let the tears flow and watch them like rain. To embrace your humanity. To embrace your divinity.

Goddess, forgive us. We are trying our best. And our efforts are beautiful.

Reflection:
Using pen and paper, write a letter of forgiveness to yourself. Start with "I forgive myself for..." and let your pen flow.

Embodiment Practice:
Place the letter from this reflection in a nonflammable container such as a pot or cauldron and light it on fire. As you watch the letter burn, breathe deeply and imagine yourself absolved from all shame. After it is incinerated, notice how you feel in your body and energy.

Day 25: I Choose Compassion

A few years ago, I led a yoga retreat in Greece, on the beautiful island of Amorgos. It's an incredible and untouched place, known for its solitude, nature, views, amazing people, and culture. This was my third visit to the idyllic island, and I was on a mission to receive healing from Vangelis, a local herbalist, essential oils distiller, and energy healer.

I had visited his and his wife's shop on my previous visits, seeing how the oils are made, hearing how they harvest wild herbs and flowers with the moon cycle, and buying as many oils as I could afford just to have the sense memory of being in their magic. I heard they conducted private healings, and was excited and nervous to book my session.

I took the long hike up the beautiful, herbaceous terrain, to their tiny village where they live and work. On the way up, I allowed my mind and heart to open to what I was needing. Here I was, living my dream, teaching yoga to beautiful people on this wondrous island, a true manifested moment, but I wasn't allowing myself to completely enjoy it. Truthfully, I was feeling burnt out. I had been working my ass off to make my current career dreams a reality. I would hustle to create and launch a new project and then move on to the next without celebration and without rest. I was in a hyper-masculine phase. Going, going, going, but not taking the time to receive the gifts of my life. I was so afraid of fucking up, of losing what I had built, that I was in a state of constant vigilance and worry.

So I knew I needed help becoming softer. Inviting in the feminine. Releasing the tension and blockages in my body that no amount of yoga, delicious Greek food, or poolside reading would fix.

So I sat down with Vangelis, in his tiny cave of a healing space, and explained to him how I was feeling. And our session began.

I closed my eyes and he started the session using words alone, bringing me into the present moment. Then, to my surprise, he asked me to tap into my sadness. Immediately, the tears started to pour. I wanted to wipe them away, but he invited me to let them be, to truly feel them.

As we tapped deeper into my personal sadness, tears flowing, he invited me to now bring my awareness to the sadness around me. He asked me if I could feel it, and I could. He said that in this world, we talk about and focus on unconditional love, love without reason, love as a currency. But we don't speak about unconditional sadness. Sadness that is a part of the fabric of existence, around us and within us at all times.

I've always felt it, ever since I was a little girl. The sadness. And trying to shield everyone else from the feeling, I've internalized it, let it eat at me. Sacrificed myself. Vangelis explained to me that my ability to tap into sadness is a superpower. He invited me to stop personalizing it, and just let it flow through me, in and back out. Not holding on, releasing the blockage.

And as I did, the tears kept flowing and flowing. He told me that this sadness is sacred, important. That when we allow unconditional love and unconditional sadness to flow through us it alchemizes to become COMPASSION. I felt it. The love and the sadness mixing together, filling my tears with healing magic. I felt myself soften, I felt myself able to truly receive, I felt true compassion. I felt my heart burst with divine love, knowing that being able to tap into this flow could heal me and help heal the world.

Sister, do you feel the sadness? It's OK to let it flow. To let go of attachment to it. To stop trying to run from it or protect yourself from it. Sister, invite the love and sadness to combine into an unstoppable flow of radical compassion.

Give yourself and others grace. Not because we've earned it, but because it is the way of the Goddess. Because it is our true nature. Because our hearts long to be open.

Your embodied and flowing compassion is the medicine to heal the world. To usher in the feminine. To rest and celebrate. To soften in peace. To connect. To truly BE your Inner Goddess.

Reflection:
How do you deal with sadness? Do you allow yourself to feel it, or do you push it away? Are you compassionate with yourself?

Embodiment Practice:
This practice is inspired by the Buddhist meditation, *Metta Bhavana*. Find a comfortable place to sit and soften or close your eyes. As you breathe deeply, tune into your heart, cultivating *metta,* or loving kindness. Imagine another version of yourself, at any age, sitting directly in front of you. Send loving kindness from your heart to hers. You are welcome to send this as a feeling, as a visual, or as words of affirmation. When you are finished, thank yourself for both giving and receiving loving kindness.

Day 26: I Am Grateful

Sister, what are you grateful for?

It is so, so easy to stew in the feeling of lack. That something's missing. That you're in heaviness, stagnation. That your heart hurts and is closed to protect you from life's bullshit. It's easy to look around and see a world that needs healing and people who are hurting. That you're in a hole that it's hard to dig your way out of.

I've been there, plenty of times. Whether I've been in deep depression or maybe have just been on my period and hangry. It's a place of heaviness, despair, and drama. It can be so hard to see the other side or to remember what it feels like to be light, present, and free.

But you have the power to turn it around with a simple tool. Take a moment, look around, and find 5 things you are grateful for. Maybe there's a pile of laundry on the floor and every time you walk past it, it feels like an insurmountable mountain of shame. But dang, girl, look at all those garments you get to choose to wear on your beautiful body! Maybe you're outside and you see a garden needing a ton of weed pulling. Shit, girl, you get to spend time in freaking nature and wow, you're going to have so many delicious veggies and beautiful flowers! Maybe your kids are whiny and you feel touched out. But aren't they the most miraculous little creations? Maybe there's a painting in your room that you loved when you chose it but now you barely see it. Isn't it a work of art? What about your doggo or kitty cat? I mean, how dare they be so cute??? Keep looking around, some of your stressors or things you take for granted could actually be your portals to gratitude!

Gratitude is a muscle. The more you practice it, the stronger it becomes. Suddenly, you can look around at this life you co-created with Spirit and this abundant Earth and even at your "failures" and you find there is gratitude everywhere.

And when you're a vortex of gratitude, you attract abundance! You see that even when life feels shitty, there is always more and more and more and more to be grateful for.

That every present moment has a literal present just for you!

And your heart bursts wide open and you think, "Wow, look at this beautiful life unfolding just for ME!"

Goddess, embrace the attitude of gratitude and feel your heart grow! Feel yourself attracting even more to be grateful for!

Feel the deliciousness that is *Santosha,* the yogic principal of contentment. And, Goddess, this is NOT complacency. Our Solar Plexus chakras are activated and when we also activate the heart, we live in our purpose, love our lives, and roll in the absolute opulence of the present moment.

Queen, it's time to stop, drop, and be grateful!

Please note, if you are in a serious mental health crisis, please seek professional support. I have, and many times! While you certainly can still develop a gratitude practice and while it can still be quite potent and powerful, you may need additional help to bring your body and mind into a safe and regulated state.

Reflection:
Set a timer for 5 minutes and list everything you feel grateful for. If the timer goes off and you are still on a roll, keep going! Keep the list somewhere you can see it on a daily basis or whenever you need a boost.

Embodiment Practice:
Choose a special person in your life, and text or call them with a special message of why you feel grateful for them. Notice how your heart feels when you compose and send the message.

Day 27: I Give Freely

There is so much magic in giving with an open heart.

When I was a young adult and in school, I worked various serving jobs. I was an absolutely terrible restaurant server. My sensitivity, which I hadn't yet understood or harnessed, combined with rude customers and workplace harassment was a terrible combination and I was constantly flustered and overwhelmed.

Although the money wasn't as abundant, I found a home working in coffee and tea shops. The customer interactions were shorter and more pleasant, and I loved all of the brilliant weirdos I worked and conversed with on the daily.

A couple years into my barista career, I was happily working at a tea shop in Chicago but was still finding customer interaction really difficult. While I could jump into a conversation about lucid dreaming, or 70s versus 80s David Bowie with my colleagues, I couldn't master small talk. The short, surface conversations felt painful and after a shift chock full of these interactions, I'd leave feeling drained.

On my commute to work, I started reading *The Seven Spiritual Laws of Success* by Deepak Chopra every day. I was certainly not feeling like a successful person, so when a friend gifted me this book, I figured it couldn't hurt.

One of the seven laws was the "Law of Giving". In this. Deepak urges you to give a gift to everyone you meet. It doesn't have to be a physical item, although it can be. But it can be a compliment, a prayer, a smile. Being a broke college student living with three roommates, this concept really opened my eyes to what giving truly means.

I decided to experiment with this and start giving compliments, silent blessings, or smiles to every customer I interacted with. The shift was immediate and palpable. Instead of feeling drained, I felt energized. People loved receiving the kind words, and I could see it shifted their presence and mood immediately. It became much easier to speak with strangers and my energy felt different.

Soon enough, management noticed as well and I received a promotion. The company was a quick-growing start-up, and I started managing shifts, helping to open new shops, and eventually worked in graphic design for corporate. I truly believe that that small shift was what it took to change my energy, and begin an upward trajectory into a more creative and aligned role.

Ultimately, it wasn't my soul's path to continue a life in the service industry, but it taught me a valuable lesson in how I hold my energy and embody giving. When I'm teaching yoga or spending time with my daughter, I take this lesson from Deepak, open my heart, and feel the amazing transmission of abundance.

Sister, giving with an open heart leads to expansive pathways unknown. Part of the shadow of the feminine is to feel beholden to and drained by constantly giving. Since it's expected of us, and part of our duties, we can start to resent it. But as we strengthen our lower three chakras, open our hearts, and CHOOSE to give freely, we realize that this form of giving is connecting us deeply to ourselves and to others. And when we are more connected, we are more loving. And as that love spreads, our life expands and our potential becomes infinite.

And when we open our hearts to freely give, we also receive. As we learned in the Root Chakra, abundance is a currency and it's important for the current to flow both ways. When we receive, we give and when we give, we receive.

And in this exchange, we embody abundance, our hearts expand, and every single person on Earth benefits from this open current of enoughness.

Goddess, give freely, and prepare to receive more than you have ever imagined possible.

Reflection:
What is your favorite way to give? Does giving help you feel abundant or does it drain you?

Embodiment Practice:
Give a sincere compliment to the next stranger with whom you interact. It can be your barista, gas station clerk, unfamiliar neighbor, etc. Notice how your energy shifts after freely giving.

Day 28: I Am Joy

Just a reminder that *joy* isn't something reserved for the weekend, holiday, or peak experiences. While joy can be found in the moments turned up to 100 it also whispers in the everyday mundanity of life.

When we pause, get curious, appreciate things as they are, drop stories and judgments and just BE, we can tap into the joy that is our birthright.

I watch my daughter in glee at a shadow, mystified at birds overhead, entranced at Dada's voice telling a story. And I tap into the bliss of simple existence by being in the seat of the witness.

I remember being a child, alone in my room, listening to a song as I lay on my back and stare at the ceiling fan. I remember giggling with my friends at sleepovers at we talked about our crushes. I remember pretending I was a mermaid in the bath, swishing my hair back and forth. I remember my mom lovingly braiding my hair or falling asleep cuddling my dad on the couch as he watched golf on TV. Spinning in circles on the playground at school until I was too dizzy to stand.

But somewhere along the way, I stopped knowing that I was enough, and started looking for joy outside of myself and the present moment. I tried finding it in shopping, drinking, too much cannabis, unconscious sex, TV shows, my phone, and other people. From ages 17-27, I was in a deep depression and an overall joyful life did not seem possible.

However, even at my darkest times, there were still glimmers of joy in my friendships, in music (thank you, David Bowie and Freddie Mercury for being my joy gurus), in fashion and creativity, in deep conversations, in nature, in dancing, and in small, beautiful moments of synchronicity. Even In the search itself.

There were a few moments of ecstatic joy. In my early twenties, before I had devotional practices in my toolbelt, I was able to get glimpses of what life could be if I was truly present by experimenting with magic mushrooms and LSD. In the right doses, these can act as medicine to zap you right out of your limited beliefs and right into the present moment. I had ecstatic moments of painting, laughing to tears with friends, listening to music, dancing gleefully, and just enjoying being in my weird and wonderful body. I don't personally feel it's a permanent solution to being present and tapping into joy, but I do attribute these experiences to helping me see, feel and know that the present moment is all that exists, and is where all the juiciness lies. This was one of the first trail markers guiding me to my spirituality.

What I needed were sustainable practices (not requiring tripping balls) that reminded me daily of who I am (divine), where I am (the present).

After intense therapy and cultivating a regular yoga and meditation practice, the more I connected to my body. The more trauma I faced and released. The more I was able to be fully present with ME. The more I expanded. The more I was able to love me. The more I found her, *Ananda,* or bliss.

Joy doesn't have to feel like tripping balls or an orgasm, the biggest laugh you've ever had, winning the big game, or traveling to an exotic locale. Joy is in the present, in a mind free from distraction, vibrating in every cell of the body and in everything around us. It's waiting for you to see, hear, and know it.

A simple breath, the delicious feeling of the Earth under your feet, the song of birds, your kitty taking a nap, the feel of your pen gliding across paper, a deep breath, looking into the eyes of someone you're connecting with... all little moments of joy that add up to a joyful life.

Sister, joy is YOURS and yours alone to claim. Joy is your birthright, joy is your frequency. The yogic body, or the *koshas,* are made up of five layers, each layer moving closer and closer to our true self, or spirit. There is the physical body, the breath, the mind, the intuition, and then the closest layer to our spirit is *Anandamaya Kosha,* or bliss. It is our true nature. Our very essence.

Sister, you ARE joy. Claim it. Follow it. Know it and sprinkle that shit around like glitter because the world needs this frequency. The world needs your joy.

Reflection:
What is something you can do every day to tap into joy? What does joy feel like in your body? How can you bring joy to others?

Embodiment Practice:
Find the posture *Anahatasana* or Heart Chakra Pose. From your hands and knees, walk the hands forward and melt your heart toward the Earth. Keep the pelvis over the knees and rest on either your forehead or chin, depending on your mobility. Breathe deeply and say to yourself, "My heart is open to joy." Hold for about 1 minute, then rest in Child's pose.

Week Five

The Throat Chakra

This week, we move into the ethereal realms with the Throat Chakra, or *Vishuddha*. Located in the base of the throat, this chakra is the first of the nonphysical chakras, embodying sound, communication, and authenticity. When it is open and strong, it sings songs from our ancestors and channels messages from Spirit. It connects us with our unique magic and allows us to share it with the world. It holds space for others and helps them feel safe and seen. It connects us to our highest selves.

I invite you to take a moment and place one hand gently on the throat (or hovering over it if more comfortable) and one behind the neck. Take several deep breaths, and focus your energy and attention on the Throat Chakra. See it whirling, a sixteen-petaled flower blue as the sea. Imagine it, bringing the love from your heart and manifesting it into sound. Gathering the wisdom and insight from your higher chakras and creating a more beautiful reality. Feel it, free, expressive, and fearless. You might fill the chakra with its sacred sound, *Ham*, by chanting it three times. Then release with a breath in through the nose, and out through the mouth.

Sister, the world needs your voice. You are here, at this specific time and place in history, to co-create a more beautiful, equitable, and feminine reality. Your voice is a superpower and you wield it with grace. Your thoughts, manifest as words, are important. Know that if you hold fear or limiting beliefs around unleashing the power of your authentic voice, you are not alone. For many centuries, women and queer people whose existences have contradicted the authoritarian and religious rule have been violently silenced. But for many of us, the time to speak up is now. We do it for ourselves, for marginalized folks, for the rise of the sacred feminine, and the good of humanity.

Throat Chakra (*Vishuddha*)
Location: Base of the throat
Energy: Communication, Authenticity, Truth
Color: Blue
Sacred Sound: Ham
Element: Ether (Space)
Overactive Chakra Symptoms: Talking too much or talking over others. Inability to hear the intuition or receive truths from others.
Underactive Chakra Symptoms: Fear of judgment. People-pleasing. Fear of standing in one's truth.
When in Balance: We are able to speak our truth and listen deeply to the truths of others. Our outer expression matches

our mind and heart. We feel authentically ourselves. We share our gifts with the world.

Connect to the Throat Chakra with:

Food: Sea Vegetables, Blueberries, Honey

Scents: Clove, Eucalyptus, Fir

Crystals: Amazonite, Aquamarine, Turquoise

Activities: Singing, Chanting, Listening to Music, Deep Conversations

Day 29: I Use My Voice

As a little girl, Spirit gave me the gift of singing. My parents took home videos of me singing and dancing before I could talk or walk. It was joyous, it was natural, it was a pure happy expression.

At age 3, I sang my first solo at Worlds of Fun, a local amusement park. It was a tongue twister of a song *I Want to Be Happy*, and I dutifully sang every syllable in perfect pitch. It was my first taste of applause. My voice gave me a sense of power and a sense of fulfillment. I might be little, but I can turn any adult's frown into a smile with just my voice. As I got a bit older, I sang in musicals, in church, at my dance school, and more. I remember my father, a man of great faith, listening to me sing, tears of pride and emotion in his eyes.

As I got even older, I became a classically trained singer and spent much of my time in high school in the music department. Around the same time, I lost my religion. I started dating and having sex and toying with drinking and smoking weed. My mind was opening, but I was in a chasm… my childhood on one side and adulthood on the other. I felt like both and neither. My father didn't know how to relate to me anymore and he was devastated with the loss of both my Christianity and my virginity. When I had the opportunity to sing a solo of *Silent Night* in a Holiday choral performance, I jumped at the chance, hoping my father would notice and would love ME and see ME again. He had tears in his eyes, but I knew they were much more complicated than those many years ago when I was young and innocent.

My father's love and approval was so important to me that I knew it wouldn't feel safe to tell my truth. I would hide parts of myself to protect us both emotionally. So I hid my voice, only sharing it with those I thought wouldn't judge me. And my voice shrank.

When I was a little bit older still, I moved in with a boyfriend with a shared love for music, impressive vocal and instrumental talent, and a massive ego. Every time I sang around the house, he would unconsciously sing over me, drowning out my voice. As a very young adult, I didn't realize it at the time, but he felt emasculated by my humble talent and couldn't bear for his girl to outshine him. And my voice shrank some more.

I stopped singing except for the occasional family wedding or funeral. I even sang a song at my own wedding for my husband and mother-in-law's first dance, and while people seemed to enjoy it, the sound levels were off and my 2-year-old nephew stood on the dance floor with hands over his ears yelling, "TOO LOUD." And my voice started to feel nonexistent.

A few years ago, in my healing journey, I attended a Throat Chakra workshop where, after some intense yoga, the instructor invited us to chant, "My voice. My choice." It started quietly but eventually crescendoed to a ROAR. Tears streaming down my face, I beat the floor with my fists and yelled the mantra like a battle cry. Afterward, in the calm after the storm, the instructor invited us around her harmonium for improvisational singing, and for the first time in forever, I let my classically trained soprano voice sing loudly with pure joy. I felt liberated and I knew the road to healing had begun. It was time for my voice to grow and grow.

Although your story may differ from mine, have you ever found yourself stifling your voice? What if your voice is EXACTLY what this world needs to heal? What if your Inner Goddess HAS to speak through YOU, just YOU and that vibration is part of a harmony that's creating a whole new Earth?

For many centuries (and still for many women in the world), our voice and our MAGIC have been absolutely hunted and squashed by the patriarchy. It has been DANGEROUS to share our voices and thus our MAGIC. We carry our ancestors, we carry our past lives within our modern bodies, so of course it feels dangerous to speak our truth and share our powerful voice.

But, Queen, it is time to let her out. We have the blood of our foremothers as a sacrifice meant to give us a safe platform to practice our magic. To whisper spells. To ROAR our babies out. To stand up for what is right. To sing just for the fucking joy of singing. This is OUR time, and it is about damn time we take our muzzles off of our Throat Chakras and FUCKING SING.

Reflection:
Have you ever felt afraid to speak your truth? What influences in your life have stifled your voice? What hidden truths do you have to share with the world?

Embodiment Practice:
Take a shower and sing your heart out. Don't worry about how you sound. Pick your favorite song to sing and let go! Bonus points if you do this publicly (minus the shower, of course) via karaoke!

Day 30: I Look Inward

When there is a lot of noise in our world, we can bring our focus inward with the practice of *Pratyahara*, or sense withdrawal. An important yogic step on the way to enlightenment, *Pratyahara* allows us to cut out the noise, and be alone with ourselves.

At any given moment in this modern world, our senses can be overly engaged. From work, to family, to the constant checking of the phone, to listening to music and podcasts, to reading books and watching TV, to the noise of traffic and sirens, our daily lives are overflowing with stimulation. It's so easy to get sucked into the chaos and unconsciously absorb this blanket of sensory input that keeps us from our own thoughts and feelings.

I remember being a little girl, in the days before smartphones, alone in my room, lying on my bed and staring at the ceiling fan. Watching it spin and whirl, I'd let my mind relax, dream, and wonder. Unburdened by the demands and distractions of adulthood, I could easily slip into this trance-like state of imagination.

The quiet, the stillness, even the boredom, was an invitation to travel into the depths of my own being. A passive exploration of inner space.

And when we turn our senses inward, we find that our inner landscape is just as vast, textured, and varied as our outer one. There is so much to explore, so much to imagine, so much to dream.

There is an inner well within us, rich with infinite waters, a direct line to source energy. An ocean of possibilities, of wonders.

As an adult, I find this state alone on a hike. In child's pose on my mat. In the dark before rest. When I'm preparing for meditation. When my breath is steady. When I'm writing. When I'm focusing only on my daughter playing quietly. When I'm truly looking at a piece of art or drinking in a beautiful song.

I dial down the noise of the world and pull from the deep well inside of me, allow myself to feel whatever comes up, and embrace it with curiosity.

And I find this stillness, the quiet, the *Pratyahara* refreshes my *prana,* or life force energy, so that I may be radically present. So that my words have more potency. So that I hear more clearly. That I'm in tune with my truth.

One of my favorite quotes from the 20th century novelist Franz Kafka is, "You do not need to leave your room. Remain sitting at your table and listen. Do not even listen, simply wait, be quiet, still and solitary. The world will freely offer itself to you to be unmasked, it has no choice, it will roll in ecstasy at your feet."

Sister, it's OK to just be. Close the book. Turn off the phone. No distractions, no obligations. Turn inward and be in your own company. Listen to the whispers of the Universe. Commune with the richness of quiet, the luxury of inner space.

Queen, there is a deep well of mystery, potential, and possibility within you. Just listen and wait for the magic of quiet. Goddess, she is calling.

Reflection:
Are you comfortable in the quiet of your own company? When you are alone, when do you feel the most serene? Do you give yourself space to just be?

Embodiment Practice:
Bhramari Pranayama, or Bee Breath, is an excellent way to quiet the internal noise, regulate the nervous system, and practice *Pratyahara*. In a comfortable seat, take deep, slow breaths in and out of the nose. Then, start the technique by breathing in deeply through the nose, then as you breathe out, simply hum a low "hmmm" sound. You'll notice it sounds like its namesake, the bee. Continue this subtle humming for several minutes, perhaps finding *Shanmukhi Mudra* by bringing the thumbs to close the ears, the index fingers to the eyelids, and the other fingers to the rest of the face. When you are finished, notice how you feel.

Day 31: I Listen Actively

Sister, let's be active listeners.

When someone is speaking to you, do you drink in the words, giving each one space in your mind, and fully immerse in the story?

More likely, like me, this isn't always the case. It's easy to space out into your own world, filter someone's words through layers of your own perception and bias, or formulate a response or rebuttal while the other person is still speaking.

The Throat Chakra encompasses communication, which can be much more complicated than we give it credit for. First and foremost, with the nature of the mind, we are constantly communicating with ourselves. From the time we develop language to the time we pass, the mind is in active inner dialogue. It spins and weaves and travels through time. There are pictures, words, memories, projections, fantasies, and more. With all of this action, it's a wonder we are able to communicate with others at all! Have you ever noticed that you've had a whole conversation with someone and have no idea what the other person even said? We can be so absorbed in our monkey minds that we hear, but we don't truly listen or understand.

The monkey mind, swinging from branch to branch or thought to thought, can also grab another's words and twist them and add meaning to them that doesn't actually exist. The perception of our own reality can be so steeped in bias due to our beliefs and individual experiences, that communication becomes messy. We twist words and tack on meaning to fit our subjective viewpoint. In this case, we were listening, but we weren't really hearing what the other person was saying.

We also can be so eager to express ourselves and be heard that when the other person is speaking, we are busy formulating our response. Maybe their words are triggering in you a similar experience and you just have to share. Maybe you don't agree with what they are saying and you are ready to argue your own point of view. While you are busy formulating a response, are you truly hearing what the other is saying?

For most of us, active listening takes work. With the nature of our busy minds, active listening can take as much effort as meditation and is in itself a form of meditation. It is absolutely worth the effort as you will see a great improvement in your relationships and intimacy. You will gain a better understanding of others. Your curiosity will grow. Judgment will lower. And your own words, when you choose to speak, will hold more potency.

There are a few key components to active listening. First, it requires an intention and desire to improve your communication. This means pausing and internally setting an intention to have a conscious conversation. Then, when you are listening, slow your breath. When you breathe deeply and slowly, it tells your nervous system to calm down and allows your mind to do the same. Next, allow yourself to be curious. When we move from a place of judgment to a place of curiosity, we invite in presence and compassion. This gives the other person space to feel safe to speak comfortably and be themselves. You can also observe their body language, tone, and energy with curiosity, giving you a fuller picture of what they are truly saying. Last, when it is time to respond, take a pause first and then speak from your heart.

Sister, when we open the door to conscious conversation through active listening, we are embracing the divine in real time. Remember. as the great spiritual teacher Ram Dass said, "Treat everyone like God in drag." As an active listener, you get to hear, see, and embrace the divinity within everyone. We also embrace our own divinity by gifting others the compassion, nurturing, and space that Goddess gives. We elevate our conversations beyond the mundane and into the sacredness of NOW. The Goddess is benevolent pure awareness, omniscient, and eternal. When we actively listen, we are embodying her spirit and inviting her magic to flow.

Reflection:
Have you noticed your "monkey mind"? What does your brain tend to focus or fixate on? When you are in conversation with others, are you truly listening?

Embodiment Practice:
Have a conversation with someone today, setting the intention to actively listen. Breathe deeply, listen and observe with curiosity and without judgment, and wait to respond intentionally and from the heart. Notice how this might differ from your everyday conversations.

Day 32: I Align with Integrity

Sister, do your thoughts, words, and actions align with your values? Are you living a life of integrity?

If you value beauty, are you thinking beautiful thoughts, having beautiful conversations, and immersing in beautiful actions?

If you value truth, are you being truthful with yourself?

If you value peace, are you cultivating peace inward and outward?

Our values are a symbol of the better world we wish to create. We long for something truer, more blissful, more in alignment with our divinity than what currently exists in our physical reality. But we will never create the world we wish to see if we don't take accountability for our own beings and align every layer of ourselves with the Goddess, with our highest selves.

When we think, speak, and act out of integrity with our Inner Goddess, we are not only betraying ourselves, but we are actively resisting heaven on Earth.

I don't share this to shame or blame, but to invite you to open your eyes to the truth that inner violence begets outer violence.

As an example, one of my greatest values has always been nonviolence. Growing up, enduring harsh words, seeing blatant violence as entertainment, and feeling the callousness and carelessness of this world wounded me deeply. I wished to live a life of harm reduction. Of awakened love.

I stopped eating animals at age 12, and went vegan in my 20s. I frequented thrift stores to reduce my blueprint, gave food to the homeless, tried my best to be a kind daughter, sister, friend, and girlfriend, spoke kind words, and gave freely.

But I was horribly violent toward myself. On a daily basis, my Inner Bully wreaked havoc on my brain and body. I would curse myself for not being good enough, smart enough, happy enough, pretty enough, secure enough, and the exhaustive list would spiral and spiral. I could shut her up with art, with kind conversations with others, with copious amounts of weed and alcohol. With dancing the night away. With eating and purging.

Instead of embodying nonviolence from the inside out, I was trying to do it from the outside in. If I do enough kind actions, just maybe I'll be in integrity and at peace with myself. Instead, I was like a vacuum for all the harm in the world, absorbing it and self-sacrificing in an effort to reduce outer harm. And it was killing me. I was not living in alignment with my true self, the self that held nonviolence so sacred. I was only perpetuating cycles of harm.

It has taken years to cultivate integrity within myself and I still slip. The bravery to sit with my thoughts has been monumental. The knowledge that my thoughts aren't ME has been a game-changer. And the ability to acknowledge that rather than being my thoughts, I am the OBSERVER of my thoughts has allowed me to reframe who I am. The observer, pure awareness, the Inner Goddess. And from my divine seat, I can witness my thoughts with empathy and compassion. And the compassion transforms the bully into the wounded little girl who is trying to protect myself and the world. And as I love on her, she softens. My inner environment is peaceful. And then I can truly live my values from the inside out.

And don't get me wrong. I make mistakes. I forget who I am. And I slip out of integrity. That is the nature of being human. But every time I notice and realign, I become stronger, more compassionate, and emit a stronger and stronger frequency of the world I wish to see.

Reflection:

What world do YOU wish to see? What values make up this ideal world? How can you live in integrity with these values and qualities from the inside out?

Embodiment Practice:

Throughout your day, notice anytime you want to tell a lie, big or small. When you notice, is it possible to change directions to align with your Inner Goddess, your highest self? For instance, when a loved one asks, "How are you?" is it possible to give a truthful answer rather than "fine"? Notice how it feels to align more with your truth.

Day 33: I Speak My Desires

Your Inner Goddess needs you to speak your desires.

At age 28, when my husband and I decided to get married and share a life together, we spent time talking about whether or not we wanted children. I wasn't sure. I always thought I would, but it honestly felt impossible to me. With a mountain of student debt, I thought I had sold my future to private loan companies, and as a sacrifice to that, had to forgo my dream of becoming a mother. I also felt lost in my life and didn't want to bring a child into that.

My husband, Arthur, is 20 years older than me and had already raised a son who at the time was 19. He said he didn't necessarily desire to do it all over again, but that he also wouldn't deny me of the chance to be a mother.

Several years into our marriage, we were both very deep into building our businesses and I was pretty sure that I could be happy and fulfilled without a child. I was finally stepping into purpose, running a business, traveling the world, making amazing connections, and gaining a lot more confidence. Arthur was also building a successful business that required 70 hour work weeks.

The topic of starting a family had been off the table for several years. In fact, we leaned into our child-free life by purchasing a condo in the hippest part of the city and filling it with modern furniture that could put a child's eye out. It supported our hustling lifestyles, was virtually maintenance-free, and was easy access to all of our favorite restaurants and entertainment.

I felt fulfilled, but eventually came to realize that I did want to be a mother, more than anything. I loved our life together but the deepest part of myself wanted more. It was in my bones, my womb, the very essence of my being.

And I was terrified. Although Arthur had initially left it up to me whether we would start a family, many years had passed and we were in very different stages of our lives. My biological clock was ticking at 35 when I started feeling this deep desire, but at 55, he could have easily changed his mind and I would have completely understood.

I was extremely nervous to have the conversation. We had decided to do this life thing together, so what if we wanted different things? And who would have to concede? Or would it break us?

As women, many of us have been conditioned not to speak our desires. Or even to not connect with the many possibilities in life outside of the societal model we are given so we don't even know WHAT we desire. We shove our desires down. We produce a palatable image of ourselves for the approval of others. We are told that our desires are selfish. That they don't matter. To keep our voices down and let the men lead. That no one will love us if they truly see us. To be small and accept a small life.

Sister, do you feel this in your throat? Does it feel blocked? Are you scared to speak your truth? Your desires?

The choice to keep your desires hidden, or to not even explore what your desires even are, is a decision to cage your Inner Goddess. To keep her small. To keep her tame. To keep her hidden. But she WANTS to come out, to burst free, and she does this by implanting within you your desires. These are the codes to a fully expressed and unabashed life. Listen to her and let her move through your Throat Chakra, the sacred portal of your desires. This shapes your world, gives it color, and aligns you with those who will co-create, appreciate, and celebrate your radical wholeness.

So I made the choice. I wanted a baby. And while it was really freaking hard to have the conversation... this person who promised to do life with me said yes. I had to accept that I desired this more than him. And that his age came with a possible shorter time on Earth with our baby and a very different retirement than he may have imagined. That we had to embrace and accept an unconventional life. But I spoke my truth and, together, we created the most beautiful being. Both of our lives are richer for it, both of our *dharmas* enhanced and more fulfilled. An unconventional life suits us. My Inner Goddess was never made to be trapped in convention anyway.

Queen, speak your desires. Speak your truth. Even if it's wild, even if it's terrifying, even if you've never seen it modeled before. Uncage your Inner Goddess, pull her through your Throat Chakra, and dive into the juicy waters of your joyous adventure.

Reflection:
What are your deepest desires? How do you desire to feel in life? What actions can you take to make your desires a reality?

Embodiment Practice:
Oftentimes, our tension lives in our neck/throat area, indicating a Throat Chakra blockage. Take a few minutes to lovingly massage your neck, alternating between rubbing and light caresses. For extra oomph, add the mantra, "My desires lead me to my highest truth."

Day 34: I Sing a Sacred Song

When I became pregnant with my daughter, I felt very interested in having a homebirth and hiring a midwife instead of doctors. After some past medical trauma where I felt silenced, humiliated, and unable to advocate for myself, I wanted agency over my potential birth and for it to feel sacred and sovereign. I also longed for consistency in care and to develop a trusting relationship with my provider.

As I was searching for a local midwife, I happened upon a company called Sacred Song Homebirth. I had the intuitive hit that this was the one. In the same day, I drew from my favorite goddess oracle deck and pulled Saraswati, goddess of music, art, and wisdom. It felt like a definite sign to reach out to Sacred Song. After an initial consultation, I knew the founder and head midwife, Amber, was the one for us.

The care was truly everything I dreamed of. Especially during pandemic times, walking into her home-like office, goats and chickens in the backyard, was always comforting. She would thoroughly answer all of my questions and provide the insight and resources for me to make informed decisions about my pregnancy and care.

I became a total birth nerd, immersed in the wisdom of midwives, doulas, prenatal yogis, and hypno-birthing. Not only that, but I was able to draw from my own well of wisdom, using all the wonderful yoga, meditation, and breathwork tools I've honed and taught through the years.

When it was time for labor, I felt prepared to focus my mind, relax between contractions, and listen to my baby. When the contractions started becoming intense, I utilized the technique I mentioned previously, *Bhramari Pranayama* or Bee Breath. It's a deep inhale and then a long, sustained hum. I knew this would help me focus my mind, relax my nervous system, and help my cervix dilate for birth. So, for hours, I hummed.

As birth became imminent and my experience more intense, the humming turned to guttural moans, growing in intensity, frequency, and volume. My cat was cowering in the corner and I'm sure I had awoken the neighbors. A final ecstatic squeal and baby was born.

After her amazing birth, it became clear that my placenta was not birthing itself. After a period of time, my midwife Amber intervened with tactics to release the placenta ranging from gentle to medical, to manual extraction which is literally reaching through my body to pull out the placenta with a hand. After this excruciating experience, it wouldn't budge and it became clear I had to transfer to a hospital for surgical help. I had to leave my sweet and healthy baby girl at home with my mother, husband, and midwife's assistant, and get help quickly as I was hemorrhaging blood.

Although I felt devastated to leave, I felt grateful for the help and knew I needed to get through this so I could get home to my baby girl. Amber was my one allowed guest at the hospital and I was grateful for her presence and advocacy.

But what I found was that unlike my previous medical trauma, I felt perfectly able to advocate for myself. I was able to let the medical staff know exactly what I needed, to communicate clearly, to say yes and no, and to do what was needed to get home as quickly as possible.

While awaiting surgery, and in a drugged haze, I was able to talk about the birth with Amber, joking about how loud I was. Although I wasn't quite embarrassed, I am a soft spoken person and have a history of being more reserved. Screaming naked surrounded by people was decidedly very much out of my comfort zone. She looked at me and said, "That's the sacred song." And I was moved to tears.

Sister, we all have a sacred song. Our powerful voices can birth babies, can express the depths of our soul, can cry, and laugh, and scream, and curse. Our voices can strongly advocate for ourselves, for others, for a better world we wish to create.

Goddess, your voice, when activated by your truth, your depth, your authenticity, your vulnerability, your emotions, is sacred. Please do not hide her. Let her out. Let her sing. Let her speak miracles and move mountains. Let the sacred feminine express through your Throat Chakra and raise the vibration of the world.

Reflection:
What would you scream to the world? What would you sing? Whisper?

Embodiment Practice:
For several minutes, try chanting the sacred mantra *Om*. This universal mantra, pronounced Aum, represents birth, life, death, and rebirth. It is the sound of the divine and of all things connected in unity. Find a comfortable seat and take a few deep breaths. Inhale deeply, then exhale a low tone with the sound *Auuuuummmmm*. Repeat for several minutes, embodying the feeling of connection to the Goddess. When you are finished, notice how you feel.

Day 35: I Share My Gifts

Sister, I invite you to share your gifts.

There is something within you that can only be expressed through you. Your DNA, your soul imprint, your story, your magic. Goddess is choosing to flow through you and needs your unique self to be the instrument of her work.

Your ancestors, their stories, their victories, their trauma, their blessings, their occupations, their instinct for survival and joy have all created the unique DNA of your body and mind. Their lives made you and your gifts possible. When Goddess flows through you, she also flows through their sacrifice, stories, and dreams. You embodying her gifts and sharing them with the world is a unique by-product of thousands of generations miraculously coming together to make you.

Your soul, with its unique imprint of past lives and personality, chose to be on Earth right here, right now. All of its experiences, wisdom, and divine missions have combined with your body to raise the vibration of this Earth. To be a light. To remember who you are. To awaken the world. It is ready and willing to be put to good use.

Your life story provides the fertile soil for your gifts to grow. Everything that has happened to you or for you, every life lesson, every bit of grief and pain, every bit of joy, alchemizing to create the most precious, nutrient-dense soil for your gifts to flourish and blossom in their unique expression.

You hold the magic, the spark, the wisdom for Goddess to flow through. Do you have the audacity to block her or will you bravely let her shine?

We block her through limiting beliefs, imposter syndrome, numbing, hiding, being too busy, settling, distracting, and self-deprecating.

We let her shine by being vulnerable, showing up for ourselves and others, working on our craft, following our joy, by feeling the fear and doing it anyway, by releasing our attachment to judgment, and by stepping out boldly.

Sister, if you are unsure of your gifts or haven't discovered them yet, know they are seeds dormant within you just waiting to be watered. Ask Goddess to flow through you. Ask her to use you. Release attachment to what that might look like, and instead, follow joy, curiosity, and that feeling in your gut that's asking you to step out of your comfort zone. When you are in alignment, you will know it.

If you are aware of your gifts, but are afraid to share them, this is your divine invitation. Choose your medium and share. Lean into the discomfort. Embrace the positive and constructive feedback and block the haters. Trust that whoever is meant to connect with your gifts will, because that is the nature of the Goddess. She is emitting a specific frequency through you, and it will reach those who are ready and willing and needing to tune in.

And if you are aware of your gifts and are sharing them with others, thank you. You are doing Goddess's work, and the more you share your gifts and your light, the more others will feel inspired to do the same. You are helping to build a world where we see, feel, and know the unique divine spark within everyone and everything. Heaven on Earth. Keep going, sister. Keep sharing.

Queens, it's time to stand together and boldly share our gifts. Let's be radically seen and heard. Let's trust ourselves and trust Goddess. Let us unleash color and magic and light upon our communities, our countries, the whole wide world.

It's time.

Reflection:
What are your innate gifts? What skills have you worked hard to learn? How can you share your unique set of talents with the world?

Embodiment Practice:
Choose a medium to share one of your gifts. Whether it's social media, in-person, or otherwise, choose a gift, and without judgment, share it with your community!

Week Six

The Third Eye Chakra

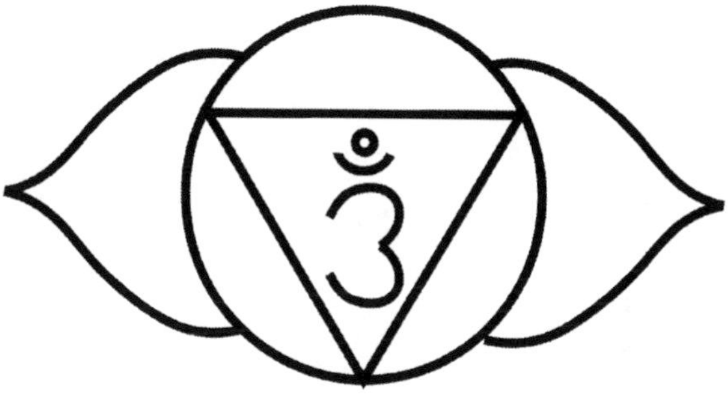

In our penultimate week, we tap into our inner mystic with the Third Eye Chakra, or *Ajna*. Located in the forehead between the eyebrows, this chakra connects us to a higher realm and wider perspective. As we step into a trusting relationship with this chakra, we hear the whispers of intuition and follow them beyond logic. We see how the pieces of our lives, and even past lives, have come together to create the perfect expression of NOW. We rely on our wisdom, see through delusion, and step into our superpowers. We co-create with Spirit, holding a vision for a healthy and loving inner and outer world.

I invite you to take a moment and place your hands on your forehead. Take several deep breaths and focus your energy and attention on the Third Eye Chakra. See it spinning, a two-petaled deep indigo flower. Visualize it holding all of the information you need. It holds your intuition, wisdom, and higher vision. It connects you simultaneously to the ancient past and to a timeless space of potential and possibility. You might fill the chakra with its sacred sound, *Om*, by chanting it three times. Then release with a breath in through the nose, and out through the mouth.

Queen, you have done so much work to fortify your lower chakras. You have aligned a beautiful foundation for your visions to become manifest. You are rooted, creative, powerful, loving, and authentic. As you embody your Inner Goddess, she invites you to tap into the subtle and mysterious realms of the Third Eye and to integrate its magic into your whole being. You are here to tap into a higher vision for humanity and use your body, heart, and soul to usher in the manifestation of something beyond beautiful. You are here to envision and manifest heaven on Earth. Are you ready?

Third Eye Chakra (*Ajna*)
Location: Between the eyebrows
Energy: Wisdom, Intuition, Connection to Non-Physical
Color: Indigo
Sacred Sound: Om
Element: Ether (Space)
Overactive Chakra Symptoms: Out of touch with reality. Overthinking. Delusions. Lack of boundaries around information being received.
Underactive Chakra Symptoms: Cut off from intuition. Rigid or limiting beliefs. Lack of purpose.
When in Balance: We see everything as interconnected energy. We manifest with ease. We trust our inner voice. We are discerning. We are curious, present, and clear.
Connect to the Third Eye Chakra with:
Food: Eggplant, Purple Kale, Purple Cabbage
Scents: Chamomile, Vetiver, Frankincense
Crystals: Lapis Lazuli, Azurite, Sodalite
Activities: Meditation, Oracle Cards, Dousing, Channeled Writing

Day 36: I Activate

Sis, it's time to open your Third Eye. If she's been sleeping, wakey, wakey, eggs and coconut bakey.

Our eyes see the world with a filter of our own perception. With bias, selectivity, and attachment. It can make us confused, unclear, unable to know if we are making the right choices for our highest selves. Without realizing it, we slip into unconscious patterns, limiting beliefs, toxic thoughts, lack of curiosity, and jadedness about life. We feel weighed down, stuck, bored. We lack trust in ourselves and play it safe. We stop imagining. Stop believing in magic. We are just going through the motions.

But the Third Eye sees clearly. She is wise. She is certain. She is clairvoyant. She gifts us not only with radical presence, but with an ability to zoom out to a much wider perspective, an inner expansiveness, and feather-light untethered bliss. She frees us from worldly constraints and connects us to the heavens. She is dreamy, wildly imaginative, pure possibility, and anchored in the deepest wisdom.

The Third Eye is not just gifted to sages and saints. She is gifted to each of us, and it is our sacred duty to wake her up, to let her see. To show that we are so much more than we have been conditioned to believe. That miracles live within the mundane. That anything is possible.

She exists beyond the construct of time. Beyond the limitations of our minds and physical bodies. She is ageless. Mysterious. And knowing.

She is our access to our inner compass. She guides and directs us into the flow of our *dharma*.

She is soft spoken. And to hear her we must quiet the noise and listen to her gentle whispers.

When we see through her, we are gifted with the curiosity and delight of a child and the deep wisdom of the crone. We are awakened. We are expansive. We trust. We connect. We flourish.

It is time for the activation. For the awakening. To ask her to open so that you can truly see.

Sister, bring your awareness to your Third Eye. Focus all of your attention on her. Feel your skin, your skull, the space around and within her. Take your eyes up to meet her. And ask her to awaken. Ask her to guide you. Ask yourself to hear her whispers. Ask her to provide the visuals, the voice, the feeling, the knowing that you seek.

Queen, it's time to pull back the veil. It's time to dive into the deliciousness of an expansive and awakened life. It's time to develop radical trust.

Are you ready? I am. Let's do this together.

Reflection:
Do you feel connected to your imagination? What do you envision for your future? Do you believe in the power of your inner vision?

Embodiment Practice:
Find a comfortable seat for meditation. Take several deep slow breaths. With eyes closed or soft, bring your awareness to the space between your eyebrows. With each inhale and each exhale, silently chant, "*Om*." After several minutes, notice how you feel.

Day 37: I Am Mindful

When I first heard of mindfulness, it seemed deceivingly simple. You mean I can just focus on one thing at a time and I'll feel happier?

But in practice, I found it extremely difficult. For instance, deep into my eating disorder, I was never just sitting down for a meal, only focused on the scent, flavor, texture, and experience. I was counting calories, worried about what the meal was going to do to my body, thinking about an argument with a friend, wondering if my boyfriend would get back to me, and so on and so on. I wasn't even there. I was everywhere, nowhere, off-center and miserable.

But with time and concentrated effort on minor tasks, I found the magic in just being here now. In slowing down. In being present. But I still had a difficult time developing mindfulness around eating.

A few years ago, while attending a workshop on macrobiotic and mindful eating, the facilitator asked us to slowly eat the beautiful fresh apple in front of us. We gazed at the apple, drinking in its color and form. We smelled it, taking in its sweet scent. Took a bite and heard the crunch and felt the texture. With eyes closed, we chewed slowly, tasting the burst of delicious flavor, and swallowed, feeling the apple slide down the throat.

Although at the time I felt healed from my eating disorder, it was truly the most present I had ever been with food. I cried tears at the pleasure, the simple magic of an apple. I felt a release in my body and the tears turned to grief over the many meals, many years lost to a distracted, frightened, and ill-conditioned mind.

Sister, are you truly right here, right now? Or is life slipping away as your mind is distracted, numb, stuck in the past, or future tripping?

Life is asking us to pay attention. To delight in her. To let things be simple. To receive the gifts that are right in front of us. She wants to be noticed, wants to be enjoyed, wants us to truly see her.

And the lesson and magic in mindfulness keep arising when I'm faced with new life challenges. When Gemma was a newborn, I felt terrible postpartum anxiety. I somehow was able to practice mindfulness and remain calm through the pregnancy, even during a global pandemic, but once she was born, I was kicked into survival mode. I was barely sleeping, my body was going through a major hormonal transformation, and I suddenly had a tiny human to keep alive.

I was exhausted but I would stay awake at night googling SIDS (Sudden Infant Death Syndrome). I would picture myself accidentally dropping her. I was worried she was too hot, too cold, and not gaining enough weight.

Catching myself in the spiral, I decided to create a signal to myself to just be here now and enjoy these precious fleeting moments. I would take a big sniff of her little head, drinking in her smell, and it would immediately draw me into the magical present. It was my reminder that we were OK. That everything in the here and now is worth celebrating. That I can let my mind relax and just be.

Queen, I invite you to truly be here. To use all of your beautiful senses to connect to NOW. This is it. This is your life. This is life itself. Soak it in. Even the mundane. Even the hard stuff. Especially the hard stuff. Be radically here and watch the magic unfold.

Reflection:
Do you feel you are present for your own life or do you feel constantly distracted? How can you be more present to your own life as it unfolds?

Embodiment Practice:
Choose a small piece of food such as a raisin or piece of chocolate. Take a moment to notice how it looks. Then take in its scent. Notice how it feels in your hand. Then place it in your mouth, noticing its texture. Slowly chew and swallow it, noticing its taste. How was this experience different than normal eating?

Day 38: I Choose Connection

Sister, are you connected or addicted?

When I first tried smoking cannabis, New Year's Eve 2001, I couldn't believe how amazing I felt. I had experimented with drinking for the past few months, and it made me feel silly and sloppy. But I remember after just a few seconds after my first hit of weed I was like, "Oh my god, THIS is my thing." It just felt right. I felt smart instead of sloppy. Relaxed instead of anxious, and curious instead of judgmental. And although it gave me the munchies, it was calorie-free, which was extremely important to eating disordered 16-year-old Lauren.

I would smoke wherever I had access and whatever I had access to, which was usually shitty stems and seeds from a shifty guy at school. I loved the smell, the feeling, the creative conversations. Listening to music. Watching interesting films. I felt sophisticated, open-minded, and free from looking, acting, and pretending to always be the good girl. I felt able to widen my perspective and able to see things from a different point of view. It was the catalyst of my spiritual awakening, a realization that life was so much bigger than the constraints of a Midwest, evangelical, suburban upbringing.

Since it seemed like such a wonderful tool and helper, instead of thanking it, putting it down, and moving on, I instead doubled down. As years passed and I became an adult, marijuana was my number one accessory and friend. When I lived on my own, I ended up using it all day long, rarely a moment without it. I would work, go to school, hang out with my friends, be alone, always high. I would buy it even when I could barely afford food and I would scrape my pipes to collect the resin and smoke it when I was out of flower. I wasn't interested in hanging out with people who didn't smoke and I clung to it tightly as an identity.

I knew in many ways, my life was falling apart. I was constantly depressed or anxious, I was in massive student debt, I felt purposeless, lost, and weak.

What I didn't fully comprehend was that I was self-medicating. That weed, while at one point helpful in opening me up and expanding my mind, became a band-aid for a hurt Inner Child, for trauma, for the power of sensitivity that I had not yet learned to own and wield. That every time I smoked, I was desperate to feel comfortable with myself, to be confident, to connect with others. But I was actually creating more and more distance between myself, my intuition, and deep connection. I had to change my relationship with it in order to be present, feel my feelings, and heal.

In Johann Hari's famous Ted Talk she says, "The opposite of addiction is not sobriety. It is human connection." I would expand that to say that it is also the opposite of self-connection and spirit-connection.

It's a deluded way to grasp at the connection we are so desperate for. It's a beast that is never quite fed, because frankly, we are feeding it the wrong food.

Sister, what are you addicted to? Your phone? "Likes"? Romance? Validation? Food? Substances? Negative thoughts? Judgment? Hot Yoga? What is it that you are TRULY seeking?

Addiction lives in the Third Eye. It blocks us from our truth, wisdom, intuition, and cosmic awareness. It keeps us playing small, confused, lost in our fears, and feeds the illusion that we are separate from everyone and everything. It distracts us so much that we cannot truly see ourselves. And when we can't see ourselves, we cannot see the Goddess because we are one in the same.

Queen, it is time to free yourself from the illusion that addiction creates and feeds. It is time to be naked with yourself. To un-numb. To feel. To heal. To be radically present. To lift the veil over the Third Eye and connect to the Cosmos. There is so much expansion, bliss, and true comfort waiting on the other side.

Goddess, for the sacred feminine to flow, we must polish the portal that is our Third Eye with deep self-connection and invite her in. As we do this together, we usher in the age of Universal Goddess connection. We are the antidote. All of us. Together.

Reflection:
Do you have any unconscious habits? Do you find yourself numbing with substances or entertainment? What could you use more discipline or space around in your life?

Embodiment Practice:
Choose one habit or substance that isn't serving you. What need is this currently fulfilling? What is an alternate healthy habit that could replace this and fulfill your need? For three days, try replacing this habit and notice how you feel.

Day 39: I See Clearly

Is your Third Eye feeling crystal clear or is it a little smudged?

Have you ever noticed that the more effort you put into finding clarity on something, the cloudier and more filtered it becomes?

We might need clarity on a creative project, a major life decision, or maybe just what to order from Postmates tonight. The weight of all of these choices when clouded with confusion can be utterly exhausting and lead to burnout and frustration.

Our society puts a lot of emphasis on hard work, deadlines, and trying and trying until something finally works. While this method has its value, it doesn't invite in the softness of the feminine, the mystery of the muse, or the divine timing of the Universe.

The mysterious feminine muse is all around us, like a cloud of fairy dust. She is waiting to be seen, to be invited in, to be channeled. But when our heads are down, our noses to the grindstone, our blinders on, when we're efforting and sweating, we don't look up to see the magic all around us. We can start to see the world through a jaded lens of burnout and we start to lose access to the sparks of joy and inspiration around us.

I have personally found that when I have space, when my nervous system relaxes, when I let go of effort, my Third Eye naturally taps into the fairy dust and ideas flow through with ease. To put it simply, a warm shower or a walk in nature tends to be a better tool for clarity than a laptop, spreadsheet or whiteboard.

In the early days after my daughter was born, although overjoyed, I felt exhausted, and at times, trapped. I was used to having a lot of space and freedom in my life, and suddenly, I had a tiny being who would scream every time I put her down and needed to nurse for hours on end. I couldn't even go to the bathroom without making arrangements. With the hormonal change from childbirth and the insane amount of love and protectiveness I felt for this child, I didn't know how I would ever process anything unrelated to her survival and happiness, let alone run a business and take on fulfilling creative projects. I felt a major lack of clarity on anything that wasn't tied implicitly to her.

But one day, when my mom came over to be with baby, I got to take a REAL shower. Not the one-minute kind where I hope and pray no one needs me for 60 precious seconds. I let the warm water wash over me, I closed my eyes, and I took a few deep breaths, and suddenly creative ideas came POURING into me. At the time, they weren't exactly welcome as I didn't have the space to manifest them, but it was a clear indicator that I hadn't lost the muse, but that I just had very little time to relax and receive her.

My decision to move back to my hometown came after a really good cry. The name for my yoga studio came while I was receiving a massage. This book, was literally downloaded into me while I was on a walk in my neighborhood, pushing the stroller.

When you truly relax into a space of receiving, the Universe is more than happy to give.

So if you're at a fork in the road, or have a creative block, or maybe are feeling clouded in general, it might be time to surrender, let it go, and trust that clarity will come when the timing is right. It might be time to schedule in some naps, nature walks, long baths, a massage, or gentle yoga. It might be time to read a book or listen to a podcast seemingly entirely unrelated to your issue at hand.

Nature is cyclical and we are cyclical creatures. We go through seasons of inspiration, effort, and rest. They are all interconnected and need to flow into each other in order to maintain flow, to avoid burnout, and to taste the many flavors life has to offer.

When we make space for conscious rest, we are making space to effortlessly receive. We receive the abundance of nature, the joy of our senses, the magic of community. We receive art, and music, and we open ourselves to receive a crystal clear inner knowing. And when the clarity and inspiration come, we know it's time to spring into action once again.

Goddess, it's time to relax, let go, and let the magic of clarity flow.

Reflection:
When do you feel most inspired? Can you think of a time when you were searching for clarity and found it? What is something you are seeking clarity on right now?

Embodiment Practice:
Take a long bath or shower free from electronics and books. Use whatever oils or products make you feel most relaxed, and give your body permission to surrender and let go. You might not receive any epiphanies. That's not the goal or point. Instead, let yourself relax without attachment or need for answers or progress.

Day 40: I Follow My Intuition

There was a period of time where I absolutely did not want children. I started really coming into my own at 29 when I took the leap for yoga teacher training, and as my career took off, I didn't see where kids fit in with my traveling yoga hippie/boss babe plan. In addition to that, my adult stepson soon moved in with us while struggling quite a bit with his mental health and the emotional toll that took on me really steered me toward that sweet and emotionally unencumbered child-free life.

But there was that damn whisper.

The little flittering something or other that would appear during meditation. Or when I had a glass too much of wine to drink. A little flittering fairy that said, "Your baby girl is waiting for you."

Nooooo, that can't possibly be! I am happy! My career is finally thriving! I'm in my *dharma*! I shooed the fairy away and did my best to drown her out.

A few years later, while on a sweet and glamorous child-free vacation with my husband and friends in Provence, after too much rosé and Sun, we had an "Oopsie".

When we came home, my period was a few days late. I took a pregnancy test and there was a faint positive. I don't know if it was the hormones or just the reality of the situation, but suddenly the mother in me turned on. I WANTED this. And BAD. But a few days later, my period came and the fantasy was gone.

But that damn VOICE was back, and this time, I listened, and listened, and listened. I just knew my baby girl was telling me that it's time.

So we made the decision to start trying, and within a couple of months, I found out I was pregnant as the world was shutting down in the early days of the pandemic. We were scared and excited, but I knew from all of the listening that baby girl had chosen here and now to come earthside. And who was I to argue?

A few weeks later, we confirmed the sex via blood test (FYI, at home drug tests are NOT for the faint of heart!) and I felt so grateful that I had trusted my inner knowing, and that although others might find it totally insane, I listened to my intuition and that of my little spirit baby.

It took me many years to hear and trust my intuition. It's damn near impossible when the mind is so full of thoughts, memories, anxieties, preoccupations and more to hear that little whisper through the noise. In yoga, we call this whirling of the mind *chitta vritti*, and the intuition, higher self, or spirit is what can be experienced and heard once we lower the volume of all the other stuff.

But, being a modern human, that's a lot to ask. There are so many distractions to occupy our minds. The 24/7 news cycle, knowing what our high school acquaintances had for dinner via Facebook, texts, demanding work, disconnection from our bodies and nature... it's amazing any of us are able to connect to intuition at all!

But the more we connect with the sensations of our body, the more we connect with JOY, the more we're able to befriend ourselves and be with our own thoughts, to be brave and confront what is real and what is just a story in our mind, to put our feet on the Earth and trust mother nature, the more the volume lowers and we can hear the magical voice that is always there at a more acceptable volume.

And then our past, the stories we tell ourselves, the ancestral trauma, and societal conditioning teach us NOT to trust ourselves. But if we can't trust ourselves, who can we trust? Marketers? Gurus? Authorities? Hell no, queen, they don't know

YOUR life! It is time to RISE UP and trust your very precious, very beautiful, magnificent miracle of the divine in human form. Trusting thyself doesn't SELL and there's no controlling a magnificent and sovereign being such as yourself. You are the chosen one and your inner voice matters!

It's time to cut the noise, to listen to her, and to let your Inner Goddess lead the way. You never know what she will birth: a daughter, a business, maybe a WHOLE. DAMN. MOVEMENT.

Reflection:
How do you hear your intuition? Does it come as words, visuals, a feeling, or a knowing? Is your intuition telling you anything that you've been ignoring?

Embodiment Practice:
If weather permits, take a walk outside. Let go of any goal or path, and instead, let your intuition guide you. Give yourself permission to attentively listen and respond, even if it takes you "off the beaten path". Go at her pace, observe with curiosity what is around you, and delight in where she takes you.

Day 41: I Am a Powerful Manifestor

Are you a master manifestor? Do you believe you can co-create the life of your dreams with the Universe? Do you believe you can find deep joy while being of the highest service to humanity?

Your thoughts create your actions and words. What you say and do creates your reality. If our thoughts are entrenched in limiting beliefs, biases, old stories, trauma, and other people's shit, it is extremely difficult to manifest the life we dream of. Hell, it can be impossible to even dream of a future worthy of your magnificent, beautiful self!

Our repeated thoughts carve deep and well-tread pathways in our minds. Over and over, we cross the same path. "I am not enough." "I am unworthy." "The Universe most certainly does not have my back." "The world is a cruel place." "I need a completely safe life." "I must be thin to be loved." "I'm never going to find joy." And on and on they go. Over and over, unconsciously our thoughts carve the paths or neuropathways. Eventually, they are all we see and everything else is forest too thick and treacherous to tread.

These thoughts and feelings are programmed into our bodies via the nervous system and filter every experience. Combined with stress and trauma, we literally embody a reality that doesn't belong to us. We live under layers and layers of illusion, forgetting who we truly are without all of the noise, the pain, the confirmation of hell on Earth.

And our life eagerly confirms this false-embodiment. We attract relationships, scenarios, jobs, entertainment, financial situations, and learning experiences that match our deeply ingrained beliefs. This confirmation bias leads us to believe that life is a casino and we were just dealt a shitty hand.

When these thoughts, beliefs, and biases are confirmed by family, culture, or society, they become a shared reality steeped in oppression. Where we are tethered not only by our own belief systems, but to the will of oppressive systems such as patriarchy, white supremacy, and unbridled capitalism. Where customs, governments, organized religions, and giant corporations all fight to capture and commodify our precious minds. And, sister, if you are not the beneficiary of privilege in these systems, it can be so very difficult to find spiritual, emotional, and physical autonomy and liberation.

But the secret is, even within bullshit hierarchal systems, only YOU own your mind. As the great musician Bob Marley sang, "Emancipate yourselves from mental slavery. None but ourselves can free our minds!"

To start manifesting the reality you desire, you must first ask, who is it desiring this life? What is the part of you that KNOWS there can be heaven on Earth? That there is a deeper truth? That there is so much more to life?

That, sister, is your Inner Goddess. She is there, even if clouded by the messiness, she is waiting and she KNOWS how damn worthy you are. That you are meant to inherit the joy, abundance, and connection you seek because deep down YOU ARE THAT.

So it's time to rewire your thoughts. To let the thoughts rewire your emotions and nervous system. To let your wise body guide the way. To visualize the life you desire. To become a vibrational match for heaven on Earth through your thoughts, words and actions. To freely offer compassion, service, and joy so that you may receive the same exponentially.

So quiet the noise. Commune with your innermost self, the one who sees a bigger and brighter future. Let her guide your thoughts. Let her enmesh with your entire being. Let her open your eyes and allow you to see the truth of who you are. That you are magic. You are divine. You can and will co-create the life you desire with her. The seed is planted, and your attention, enthusiasm, beliefs, and aligned actions water and nurture this seed. Visualize with her your blossomed life. And let your essence, your fragrance, attract more and more joy. More freedom. More lightness. Heaven on Earth.

Queen, go forth and manifest!

Reflection:
How would you like to feel in your life? What does your ideal daily life look like? What is something big you'd like to manifest?

Embodiment Practice:
Find a comfortable seat for meditation. Take several deep breaths and notice your physical body in space. Bring into your mind's eye what you would like to manifest. Notice it in detail. Notice how you feel in the process of manifestation and how you feel once it is your reality. Let your body fill with this feeling as though what you seek is already real. Bring into your heart the wonderful ripple effect of this manifestation in all that it touches. Allow yourself to feel supported by forces seen and unseen. And then release your manifestation to your Inner Goddess, inviting her to create with you, and deeply trusting things will unfold in their own time. Fortify the manifestation with a cleansing breath, breathing into the nose, and out of the mouth.

Day 42: I Am a Mystic

Darling, you are a powerful mystic.

Your vision, your insight, your connection to the Universe is strong, direct, and vast. You see behind and between worlds. You live in the grey. Your faith is great and your mind is open. You are a direct line to Source and the creator of universes. You pull inspiration from the ethers and alchemize it with your spark to birth what this world truly needs.

You see the light and the shadows and know they are one in the same. You hold pain and joy and call it beauty. The lines between past and future blur and you know that there is just now. Your eyes are both fresh in curiosity and wonder and seasoned in wisdom and knowledge.

Delusions and illusions crumble before you and you are left with only truth. You see all possibilities, all potentials. You have a deep knowing that there is so much more than our eyes can see. That we are all connected. That we all are mystics.

You step boldly into your power without grasping or owning as you know it is an infinite source that flows through you. You know the vessel is temporary but the flow is immortal.

Mystic, you dance in nature, you delight in stillness. You soak up the light of the moon and drink in the deliciousness of the dark. You're a magnet for miracles and a magnet for other mystics.

You boldly travel to other realms. Swim in their waters. Commune with their people. Taste their magic. Learn of their medicine. You heal yourself and bring back the medicine to heal others. You are an inner and outer world traveler. An astral projector. A dream dancer. A celestial being.

You connect with visions through the Third Eye and bravely pull them down to your root to ground them into reality, your womb to nurture them, your belly to transform them with inner fire, your heart to amplify them with passion, and your throat to sing them into the world.

You are a witch, a sorceress, a sage, a saint, a yogini, a medicine woman, a healer, a queen. In many lives past you have opened your eyes and brought magic into this world. It is time to wake up in this lifetime. To tap into your magic. To be a visionary. To boldly connect space and matter. To be a bridge between worlds. To own being Goddess manifest.

Goddess, wake up. Open your eyes. All three of them. The time to remember your power and purpose is now.

Reflection:
Do you feel your Third Eye is open? What do you see in the future for yourself? What do you see for humanity?

Embodiment Practice:
Find Crocodile pose by lying on your belly and placing your hands under the Third Eye. Let your body relax and invite in deep breaths. As you inhale, say to yourself, "I trust my inner vision." As you exhale, "I am magic." Repeat for several minutes until you feel complete.

Week Seven

The Crown Chakra

It's coronation time! We've made it to the final week of this journey as we embrace the Crown Chakra, or *Sahasrara*. Located on top of the head, this chakra is a direct channel to Source, the Universe, and our Inner Goddess. With the rest of our chakras aligned and balanced, flowing with the sacred feminine, we commune with our Creator, its creation, and our highest selves. We know we are above or below no one. That there is so much more than our perceived physical reality. That our existence is deeply connected to everyone and everything. That we have a sacred and holy purpose. That we are infinite light beings. Spirits embracing a human experience.

I invite you to take a moment and place your hands on the top of your head. Take several deep breaths and focus your energy and attention on the Crown Chakra. See it spinning, white and lavender, infinite petals connecting to Source. Feel it sparkling with divine energy, filling you with all of the stars in the Universe, connecting you directly to Goddess. Let yourself surrender to its all-loving and all-knowing state. You might fill the chakra with its sacred sound, *Om*, by silently chanting it three times. Then release with a breath in through the nose, and out through the mouth.

Sister, let us celebrate as we dance with the divine. Let's call in our angels, talk to Goddess, and go full woo-woo. Let us heal our wounds around religion, bypass middlemen, and step fully into our power. Let us KNOW that we have everything we need within us. Let us KNOW that we are always whole. Let us KNOW that our Inner Goddess is enmeshed with us, available anytime we need her. Let us know that we are LOVE. And let us CELEBRATE our journey home to Self.

Crown Chakra (*Sahasrara*)
Location: The top of the head
Energy: Cosmic Consciousness, Divinity, Unity
Colors: Violet and White
Sacred Sound: Silent Om
Element: Ether (Space)
Overactive Chakra Symptoms: Obsessive or myopic thoughts. Superiority. Lack of connection to what makes us human.
Underactive Chakra Symptoms: Disconnection from ourselves and others. Going through the motions. A feeling of meaninglessness.
When in Balance: Our minds and spirits align. All lower chakras are aligned and balanced. We see beauty and connection in existence and know we are divine.

Connect to the Crown Chakra with:
Food: Cauliflower, Coconut, Parsnips
Scents: Myrrh, Lavender, Spikenard
Crystals: Clear Quartz, Amethyst, Celestite
Activities: Prayer, Spiritual Study, Sleep, Yoga

Day 43: I Revel in Space

Are you giving yourself enough grace and space to connect with Source?

In a world that is so full of distractions, illusions, and shiny objects, our energy bodies can get so bogged down with heaviness and debris that it becomes very difficult to hear Spirit. But Spirit, Source, the Universe, Goddess, is always speaking.

As humans, we become very myopic and obsessive about our own lives. Our schedules, our problems, our relationships, our emotions, our thoughts, while important, can become an amalgamation of distraction and heaviness that blinds us, and veils our truth, expansiveness, and connection.

We magnify this heaviness and tunnel vision with our obsession with technology. We limit our vision to tiny screens that hold vast information. We scroll and let the screen hijack our thoughts, emotions, and energy in trade for a glimmer of connection.

While the screens in and of themselves are not bad, after all they are merely a tool that can be wielded with skill and intelligence when used consciously, it is important to exercise discretion and to create healthy boundaries around them.

So, sister, I invite you to remember our smallness. We are tiny intelligent beings, tethered by a magical force called gravity to a spinning orb of life, orbiting around the Sun, in a galaxy of 100 thousand million stars, in a possibly infinite Universe, or even Multiverse that is largely empty space.

I also invite you to remember your largeness, your expansive Universe within. At a quantum level, we are space and we are potential. We are atoms and we are empty space for the potential to dance within. There is literally space all around us and within us.

Sister, when we zoom out far and we zoom way in, we know that space prevails.

And beyond our incarnation as human, our embodied light, we are souls who thrive in expansiveness and space. We are ethereal beings who are unlimited by the physics of this plane. We are pure consciousness that truly knows no bounds. Pure consciousness that is connected to everyone and everything.

So, of course when our jobs suck, and we're in shitty moods, and our relationships are stressful, and we're filling our empty space with scrolling, numbing, or anything else that doesn't bring us closer to our spacious and blissful nature, we feel trapped. We feel claustrophobic. We feel clenched.

Queen, I invite you to remind yourself again and again of your true spacious nature. I invite you to take really deep breaths and to notice the space between those breaths. I invite you to be totally present to the love around you, whether it's a flower selflessly emanating its fragrance, or a kitty curled up in your lap. I invite you to take breaks when things feel overwhelming. I invite you to consciously make space each and every day to connect with your true essence, to move toward joy, to daydream, to meditate, to dance.

I invite you to purify your aura, to cleanse away the heaviness of life and other people's stuff that you don't need to carry. To consciously wash it away with water or to cleanse it with smoke, to laugh, to cry, or simply to cast the heaviness away with your own unique prayer or spell.

I invite you to take out the headphones, to cross out any to-do's that aren't urgent, and to release things that drain your energy. To slow down. To give yourself grace so that you can gift yourself space.

And in this space, we realize we are "plugged in" to the divine. We have unlimited access to Source.

Queen, in this space, know who you truly are. An angelic facet of the gem that is Goddess.

Reflection:
When do you feel most spacious? Does your energy ever feel like it needs to be cleansed? What is your favorite way to slow down?

Embodiment Practice:
At any point in the day where you feel crowded by business, stuck energy, or other people's "stuff" try this simple ritual. Wash your hands with warm water and soap, saying to yourself in your own mind, "I deeply wish to release anything that isn't mine. I reclaim my own energy." Visualize the release of this energy down the drain and take a deep breath to draw your own energy back to you.

Day 44: I Am Authentically Spiritual

Sister, your connection to the divine is personal, unique, and direct. Your spirituality doesn't have to present in any specific way for it to be a solid force in your life. You get to celebrate, communicate with, and seek support from Source in any way that feels authentic to you. You have the power.

When I was little, I had an unquestioned faith in Christianity. I was taught that Jesus was the literal son of God, died for MY sins, came back to life and ascended to heaven. That I was a sinner and that all I had to do to be forgiven and avoid hell was to ask Jesus for forgiveness and to live in my heart. That Jesus preached about love. That he cared for the meek and the poor. That anytime I needed him, I could pray and he would answer. That the end times were coming soon and that Christians would ascend to heaven and everyone else would live in torment. That this was THE only way.

I, of course, did not want to go to hell. I faithfully attended Sunday school, was super down with the love and compassion thing, could barely contain my excitement to be baptized, tried to "save" all my friends, and dutifully prayed every night. It filled my heart and I felt whole.

But as a teenager, I noticed the hypocrisy in the church. The politicizing of the religion. The lack of love for the poor, immigrants, and queer people. I learned of the Roman Empire and Catholic Church stamping out all traces of the sacred feminine, branding Mary Magdalene a whore rather than the holy consort of Jesus, throwing away books of the bible, twisting the words of Jesus (or in actuality, his real name Yeshua, or Joshua!) for power. I learned of the Crusades, manifest destiny, the witch burnings, and the current state of the church which seems divorced from the teachings of Jesus, the historical context of the bible, and the similarities between Christianity and other Eastern religions.

Upon this realization, I felt consumed with grief and felt a hole in my heart where Yeshua once was. But I also felt freed to find my own understanding of the world and of God. I eventually embraced "not knowing" and enjoyed learning about how other people live, what they believe or don't believe, and embarked on a journey to connect with Source again in my own way and form a belief system based only on my direct experiences and deep-seeded love.

Many years later, after a long personal spiritual journey and becoming a spiritual teacher myself, I took a week of sabbatical and stayed in a tent at an Ashram in the Bahamas, studying yoga and meditating all day, mostly in silence. The silence was only broken by a daily *kirtan,* or chanting practice, with a renowned *kirtan* artist who wove in beautiful storytelling of Sita and Ram, the Hindu Goddess and God who are greatly revered and worshipped through *Bhakti Yoga,* the Yoga of Love and devotion, often expressed through chanting, or song. The monkey God, Hanuman, a devotee of Sita and Ram, is often depicted peeling his heart open to reveal the divine couple within it. While I loved the singing and the stories, Sita and Ram never quite penetrated my heart.

I booked a "spa" service called *Shirodhara* which is an ancient ayurvedic practice where you relax on your back while the practitioner pours a carefully selected and warmed oil onto your forehead and it drips down your hair. It was said to reduce stress, and I was in a period of growing my business and not taking great care of my body, so it seemed like the perfect fit.

At first, I was surprised at truly how relaxing this felt. I softened and let the oil slowly drip down my forehead. After awhile, I suddenly felt transported to a different time and place. I can't exactly describe the experience, but I felt I was Mary Magdalene, and was receiving *Shirodhara* from Jesus (or Yeshua) himself. I felt deep and profound love for him and great power in myself. After the service, totally blissed out, but puzzled, I made my way back to the tent to rest. Later that evening, while practicing *kirtan*, tears of love streaming down my face, I pictured my heart opening, like Hanuman, with Yeshua and Mary nestled in. While I do not define myself as a Christian or follow any one religion or dogma, I felt my childhood Christianity wound healed with the addition of the sacred feminine.

Sister, there are as many ways to connect with Source as there are people in this world. You are on your own journey, and no government, church, or one person can define it for you. You get to commune with Source, question the world, choose your sacred practices and rituals, and express your divinity however you choose, or however it chooses you. You get to dive into spirit and dance with her in whatever weird way feels best. You don't need a priest. You are the priestess. You don't need a monarch. You are a queen. You don't need a bible. You have a Crown Chakra and a journal. Goddess, this is your journey and you get to travel in whatever damn way you please.

Reflection:
Were you raised with religion? Who resides in your heart? What is your current relationship with Spirituality?

Embodiment Practice:
I invite you to explore a prayer of gratitude to whomever you feel comfortable praying to. It may be a deity, the Universe, or maybe your Inner Goddess or Highest Self. There are no particular words or structure needed. Do what feels natural and authentic to you.

Day 45: I Am Truth

We are shapeshifters. Throughout our lives, we wear many hats, take on many roles, and are constantly shifting and changing. I've been a daughter, sister, singer, child, Christian, student, dancer, patient, friend, agnostic, designer, nanny, shopgirl, barista, wife, traveler, entrepreneur, yoga teacher, spiritual teacher, and mother. How I spend my time, what I am thinking, where I am, what I am feeling, how I look, what I wear, and what I know are in a constant shift.

But if I am always changing, then who am I?

One time, in high school, I was at my friend's house getting high and watching a favorite childhood movie, *The NeverEnding Story*. In the movie, the main character, Bastian, gets tangled into a world of fantasy, surrounded by mythical creatures and on a mission to save Fantasia. I hadn't seen it since I was a child and I remember the puppets and special effects seeming so vivid, so real. But on second watch as a teenager, I noticed that the dragon Falkor's mouth didn't match up with the words. And that the special effects looked so rudimentary.

For some reason, this spun me into an absolute panic. This movie, this FANTASY, that at once seemed so vivid and real, now seemed cheap and fake. I wondered why I remembered it so vividly one way, when in reality it was another.

It reminded me of growing up, being certain that the world was one way. That things were very simple, that there is one God to connect with, that if I just accept him into my heart I will be eternally safe and rewarded. And merely months before this viewing, my worldview shattering, letting go of evangelical Christianity, and realizing I have no idea what the fuck is going on. When I looked back at the reality I had absorbed as a child, I realized the mouth didn't line up with the words.

Then I wondered, who am I? I had always felt so sure of the answer, but I was no longer sure. I also had a distinct feeling of claustrophobia. Of being trapped in my own skin. I suddenly felt so alone, knowing I was the only one to ever see out of my own eyes. And I wondered, if my perception is always changing, and I'm getting older, and nothing really ever stays the same, then who the F is this "being" looking through these eyes and having these thoughts? What is even real? And am I (whoever that is) entwined in a world of fantasy like Bastian?

It's no wonder that my stoned and panicked teenage thoughts eventually led me to a deep curiosity and study of philosophy, particularly in the yogic tradition.

In many texts, and in many ways, the sages, mystics, and seers all came to the same conclusion. I am not my body, my thoughts, my emotions, my beliefs, or my roles. Those things are always changing. I am that who observes these changes. I was never born and I will never die. I am the seer, the observer, the spirit. Truth is my identity and everything else is an illusion. In layman's terms, I am mother f*cking DIVINE!

The ancient Vedic text, the *Taittiriya Upanishad,* describes the body as comprising of 5 sheaths, or layers, almost like a nesting doll. The outermost layer, *Annamaya Kosha,* is your physical sheath. The next is *Pranamaya Kosha* or the energy sheath. Then comes *Manomaya Kosha,* the thought layer. Followed by *Vijnanamaya Kosha,* the wisdom layer. The innermost layer, the one closest to the true self is *Anandamaya Kosha,* the bliss layer. Notice, that each layer contains the word "*Maya*", which in Sanskrit means "magic" or "illusion". Your physical body, your energy, your thoughts, your wisdom, and even your bliss, don't quite touch who you truly are. You are SO MUCH MORE. You are EVERYTHING.

It is so easy to forget this, but when the body is relaxed, the mind becomes still, and we drop into source energy, the same epiphany always arrives. That YOU are the one you've been looking for. You are connected to everyone and everything. You are blissier than bliss. Truth is your identity, *Sat Nam*, and everything else is simply a light show, a fantasy, Earth school, heck, maybe even a low-budget 80s fantasy movie.

Sister, you are a Goddess. You are infinite. You are truth. It's time to own it.

Reflection:
How do you deal with change? Do you embrace it, or do you cling to how things are? Are you aware that you are not your body or even your mind? Who are you truly?

Embodiment Practice:
The Observer Meditation invites you to be a curious and compassionate witness to your mind. Find a comfortable seat, deepen your breath, and close or soften your eyes. Bring your awareness to your thoughts. There is no need to change them, judge them, or chase them. Allow yourself to watch them as though they are clouds shapeshifting and passing through the sky. After a few minutes, ask yourself, who is the one observing these thoughts?

Day 46: I Am Divinely Guided

Sister, you are divinely guided. Did you know that you have a host of angels, guides, and ancestors who have your back? Who hold your sacred mission of this lifetime closely and guide you on your path? When you are feeling unclear, uncertain, in pain, in sorrow, or lonely, you can call on your spirit team to remind you of your sacred mission and your great capacity for love and connection.

When I was little, I had an intense fear of aliens fueled by summers of watching daytime talk shows like *Donahue* where the hot theme was alien abduction. I also was very concerned about demons and Satan, learning about them in my church. Every night, I would pull the covers over my head and pray for angels to surround my house and protect me from these dark and unseen forces. They were basically my bodyguards called upon only in fear.

As a young adult, freed from the tethers of organized religion as well as my fear of aliens and demons, I hadn't called on the angels in quite some time. I was deep in exploration of what spirituality even meant to me and felt tied to agnostic rationality. But I was suffering. In a spiral of depression, confusion, and sickness, I was feeling sick of my own shit and desperate for a change. I knew it was time to dig deeper and connect to something bigger so I prayed, to whoever might be listening, for help, direction, and clarity.

Soon after, I happened upon a nearby Reiki, or Japanese energy healing, training. I felt strangely drawn to it although I had very limited exposure to or knowledge of energy healing. A few years earlier, after a headbanging injury from a dance gig in *The Rocky Horror Picture Show*, a castmate gave me Reiki and not only did my pain subside, but he also suggested I might need to heal my feminine… Curious.

So although I barely had two nickels to rub together, I applied to the training hoping I could receive a partial scholarship to cover the cost. To my delight and surprise, my application and scholarship were approved! I spent the training, set in a beautiful garden, learning about chakras, white light energy, sacred symbols, and the power of energy healing. I was so grateful my intuition led me there, and I felt for the first time ever that I had made a wise investment in my spirit.

During one of the healing sessions, a fellow student said she saw me sprouting beautiful blue butterfly wings. In tears, I hoped with everything I had that it was a sign that I could grow, heal, and feel at home with myself.

At the end of the training, during what's called an "attunement" or a ritual to receive the Reiki energy, the teacher guided us through a meditation. As she had us visualize a stairway leading us to a door, she said that our spirit guide would be on the other side. At the moment, I thought this was a hilarious notion and she must be out of her mind. Although my intuition led me to this training and I enjoyed it, I still felt very tethered to my agnostic, ex-Christian, nonreligious, no BS form of reality.

But lo and behold, I opened the door and there stood before me a giant anthropomorphic white rabbit named Raul. WTF???

Raul was playful, loving, joyful, and connected me to my Inner Child. As I opened the door and he appeared so large, I noticed I was child-sized. He was here to help me integrate the wonder, spirit, and belief of my childhood with the sovereignty and open-mindedness of my adulthood. In other words, he was here to bring the magic.

After the training, I would call upon Raul when giving Reiki to someone and would sometimes imagine myself laying on his soft belly when I was feeling extra lonely or sad.

After a couple years, I called upon Raul less and less, eventually forgetting him.

But in the depths of my yoga teacher training, he made another appearance. Deep in meditation, I suddenly felt out of body. Floating in space, surrounded by stars. Suddenly, Raul appeared in front of me and his eyes were glossy black orbs filled with infinite stars. Telepathically, he told me to look at my own eyes, where I saw the same. And we both dissolved into millions of tiny stars in an infinite universe. Pure bliss and oneness. I was awoken back into the *shala*, tears streaming down my face, to my teacher singing *This Little Light of Mine*. And I laughed in joy, knowing it was a wink from Raul.

Since then, I've had many other encounters and interactions with my guides. And while I might call on them for protection, I also look for their signs that I'm on the right path. I know they answered my prayers in the depth of my despair and lit my path to deep healing and a strong spiritual knowing. I now call on them to help me stay in the path of my *dharma*, or soul's purpose, and live in compassion and love.

Sister, you have a spirit squad too, and they are ready and willing to answer your prayers. Your spirits, your guides, your angels, your ancestors, your totem animals (and heck maybe even some aliens) are cheering you on! Keep your eyes open. Keep your childlike wonder, magic, and imagination turned on. Notice their signs, their guidance, their winks and nudges. They are here to support your sacred mission.

Goddess, you are divinely guided.

Reflection:
Do you find yourself often seeing repeating numbers like 111? Or maybe there is an animal you often see when you're in need of direction. Do you believe in spirit guides, angels, and ancestral guidance?

Embodiment Practice:
Choose an animal and ask Goddess to show you this being whenever you are on the right path. Keep your eyes open and notice every time this animal appears. Trust that Goddess has your back and that you are in the flow of your soul's purpose.

Day 47: I Have a Sacred Duty

What if your incredible soul CHOSE to come to Earth at this time? Beyond the limitations of the physical body and this earthly plane, you made an agreement with Source to be here now, knowing the scope of experiences you would be receiving in this lifetime. Knowing that you are here to shift this plane with your presence, impact the collective with your gifts, and fulfill a sacred duty that can only be channeled through YOU.

What if, prior to this life, you chose your parents, your birthplace, your astrology, your struggles, and your circumstances all so that you could be in the perfect position to fulfill your soul contract?

What if you were never a victim of your own life, but an empowered spark of the divine here to help raise consciousness and impact others in only the way YOU can?

What if you were BORN with this knowledge, but given amnesia from a society of people who are asleep, with heels dug into a mirage of reality?

What if it was your sacred duty to REMEMBER and embody your soul's purpose, or *Dharma*? To break free from the fog of forgetting who you are? To step into your own power and gifts?

What if embracing your radical wholeness and embodying your Inner Goddess is exactly why you are here right now?

Sister, this journey of exploration through all parts of yourself has invited you to step into a fully expressed Queen. To see, feel, hear, and know that all parts of you deserve to come to the surface. And not to BECOME radically whole, but to REALIZE you already are. And did you know this sacred journey isn't just for your own healing and remembering? By you stepping into your wholeness and bringing ALL of you to the table, you become a siren of awakening. You came here to

REMEMBER. To ACTIVATE. And to ELEVATE all of humanity with your siren's song. To create heaven on Earth. To usher in the rise of the sacred feminine and heal the toxic masculine.

Sister, you have a gift that only YOU can channel through your being. Your DNA, circumstances and experiences have braided together to create a powerful conduit for Goddess. Your Inner Goddess knew you were ready to embody her, and through that, you will discover, nurture, and birth your purpose.

If you are ready to unlock your soul's purpose, your body holds the keys. She was designed and shaped into the perfect vessel. She already knows, and it's simply your job to remember and then be brave enough to respond.

Sister, tune into your body and ask her these questions. Let them flow and let your mind be curious rather than judgmental or limiting. What brings you the most joy? When do you feel most in flow? What are you good at? How do you like to serve the world? If money wasn't a factor, what would you do with your life? When do you feel most free? When do you feel most satisfied? What makes your heart expand? When do you feel most connected? What do you find most beautiful? What are you here to share?

Another key way to tap into infinite Source energy and your specific *Dharma* is to ask Goddess to flow through you.

When I am nervous. When I am unsure. When I am disconnected. When I am in my own way. I say a simple prayer, "Dear Goddess, please flow through me. Use me however you must. I trust that whatever flows is in service to the highest vibration of compassion, truth, and love." And then, I take a deep breath and just ALLOW and ACCEPT whatever comes.

Thank you, Goddess, for flowing through me. Thank you for helping me remember who I am and why I am here. Thank you for awakening our hearts and activating our spirits. Thank you for my struggles, my story, and my circumstances. Thank you for the opportunity to be here on Earth right now. To fulfill my sacred duty.

Reflection:
Imagine choosing your life's path before incarnating on this Earth. Why would you choose your parents? Your location? Your burdens? Your gifts?

Embodiment Practice:
When you feel you are getting in your own way or are nervous, use my prayer from above. "Dear Goddess, please flow through me. Use me however you must. I trust that whatever flows is in service to the highest vibration of compassion, truth, and love." And then, take a deep breath and just ALLOW and ACCEPT whatever comes. How does it feel to surrender and let Goddess flow through you?

Day 48: I Connect with My Inner Goddess

Sister, can you feel her? Your Inner Goddess? Can you feel the way she holds you in Mother Earth's safety? The way she whispers to your womb, lights your inner fire, expands your heart with love, fills your words with beauty and truth, opens your eyes to divine wisdom, and is your direct line to Source?

She is of the highest vibration of love, light, and compassion. She lives within earthly and celestial realms. She is timeless. She is infinite. She is abundant. She is joyful. She is EVERYTHING and she is YOU.

She chose your DNA, your earthly vessel, your gifts, your talents, your voice, in this lifetime and every lifetime.

She is the big kahuna, your BFF, your mother, your sister, your fairy godmother and she is YOU.

She is the ultimate guide, the ultimate truth, she is *shakti*, she is the divine dancer and the dance.

If the idea of her seems illusive, know that you can meet her, open up the divine line of communication, and merge with her in divine embodiment.

Reflection:
It's time to meet your Inner Goddess. Now that you have had several weeks of embodying her, what do you think she looks like? What would you like to ask her? How can you stay connected after this journey?

Embodiment Practice:
Take a few moments to get comfortable and prepare for a guided journey to meet your personal Inner Goddess.

Light a candle. Grab your favorite crystal. Put on some high vibe music and come back. I'll wait!

As you're reading, take deep expansive breaths. Let your mind completely relax and allow yourself to easefully imagine this journey.

Visualize yourself walking through a beautiful forest with trees everywhere, morning light pouring through their leaves. You're walking barefoot on a warm dark path. This path leads you to a shallow pool full of healing mineral-rich mud. Alone and completely safe, you allow yourself to disrobe and enter in the pool, gently rubbing the warm mud all over your body. You take in its healing properties and feel its nurturing energy. After your whole body is covered you make your way out of the mud back to the path, the warm Sun drying the earth on your skin.

Walking further, there is now in front of you a creek of crystalline water flowing over glittering rocks. The water is the perfect temperature, and you allow yourself to wade into the water washing off the earth and washing away anything that's weighing you down, allowing yourself to see the purity of who you are. You feel at flow and perfectly at peace.

You emerge from the water and find yourself back on the path. After a short journey you notice a beautiful and inviting fire. As you sit at the campfire you gaze into its flames, you feel them warming and drying your skin. The fire reminds you of your own confidence, your own will, your own determination, your inner spark.

As the fire dies and your body is dry you find yourself back on the forest path. Notice what you see around you: flowers, trees, birds. You find a clearing full of a soft green grass and gentle pink flowers. You sit down, and as you breathe, you simply allow the breeze to caress your skin, you feel the air dance around you and you feel expansion of your heart. You feel oneness with the forest around you.

When you're ready to continue your journey, you are back on the path now leading you out of the forest and onto a sandy beach. The Sun is starting to set as you settle on the water's edge feeling the ocean breeze and smelling her salt. You allow yourself to listen to her waves. They rise and fall just like your own thoughts, just like your own emotions. Allow the waves to soothe you. Hear the ocean whispering to you.

As the Sun sets and stars start to appear you lie on your back and gaze up at the sky seeing glittering galaxies, and you feel almost as though you're dissolving and becoming the sky. You feel yourself on this Earth floating in space and one with the Universe.

You soften your eyes for sleep. In the darkness of sleep, notice what you see around you. What environment has your dream taken you to? Notice the sights, sounds, the colors, and smells. You know you are about to meet someone very important to you. Your Inner Goddess is about to arrive. Watch her as she walks toward you. She is now right in front of you. Notice what she looks like. Ask her her name. Ask her what she is here to teach you. What she is here to help you embody. Allow yourself to be with her. To simply be or to ask questions. Let her hold you.

Send her your deepest gratitude and invite her to become one with you, enmeshed in every cell, every layer of your being. Allow yourself to embody pure love, unbridled joy, inner knowing, truth, sovereignty. Feel yourself rooted, in flow, strong and capable, open-hearted, able to speak your truth, trusting your intuition, and always open to Source.

Now feel your body back in your current space. Allow your breath to deepen. Know that your Inner Goddess, who is an expression of you, is there any time you need her. You don't need a priest, a shaman, a healer or a middleman. She is you and you are her. She is here to help you lead with love, to invite in softness, to usher in a whole new way of being. Not just for yourself but for Humanity. A softer gentler way. A wilder way. An ecstatic, orgasmic way. A harmonious way. A sacred way.

Call on her whenever you need.

Day 49: I Am Divine

Sister, know that you are divine incarnate.

Your body, your breath, your mind, emotions, and heart are a temporary and beautiful song of spirit.

Your soul has sung many songs before this lifetime and will sing many after.

Some are complex, some are simple, some bright and some wistful. They are all beautiful.

When you close your eyes, breathe deeply, and observe the song, you are in the seat of the soul. You realize you are the musician, not the song.

And the musician can change the song at any moment. She can choose an expansive, joyful, feminine, powerful, connected, and inspiring symphony of a life.

Sister, your patterns, your wounds, your body, your habits, your adventures, your life story, while important and beautiful, are not you. They are temporary, ephemeral, and meaningful works of art.

You are so much more than that. You are infinite. You are pure awareness. You are pure joy. You are God and Goddess. You are the stars and the sky and the ethers and the Earth. It is all within you and you within it.

Separateness from the divine is both an illusion and a lie. You don't need a priest. You don't need a pastor. You don't need a middleman. You have free and direct access to the divine because you are divine.

You may forget over and over. And the feeling of separation is devastating. But listen to your longing. Let it guide you back. Let yourself remember again and again that you are Goddess manifest. You always were and you will always be. Nothing can change that and nothing will.

The more you love your life's song, the more you embrace the authenticity of who you are, the more fully expressed of a life you live, the more you embody the Goddess. You are her and she is you, radically whole.

You are bliss, creation, power, holiness, and abundant. You are EVERYTHING.

We are above not below anyone. We are all in this together. So we keep our feet on the Earth, we celebrate our incarnations, and we remember who we, all of us, truly are.

The more you awaken to this truth and dance in it, the more you can sing a song of purpose and expansion. The more beautiful the song. And when other divine souls hear your song, they remember themselves too.

And soon enough, the whole world is singing in harmony. We are all in purpose, all connected, all supported, all in radical peace.

Do you see it, sister? We're all in this together. Keep going. Keep remembering. Keep embodying your Inner Goddess. We need you. It's time to rise!

Reflection:
Take a few moments to journal about your 7-Week embodiment journey. What were the biggest challenges you overcame? How have you grown? How have you embraced and embodied your Inner Goddess?

Embodiment Practice:
Sister, Congratulations! It's time to CELEBRATE! Take a bath full of crystals, oils, and flowers. Drink cacao and dance with your sisters. Take a long ass nap. You do you. Just make sure to take some time to pause, vibrate in joy and pride, and treat yourself like the Goddess you are!

Conclusion

Goddess, it has been an absolute honor to spend this time with you. It is my deepest hope that you've found a sense of support and structure as you explored, embraced, and embodied your holiness, your Inner Goddess. I am so excited to see how this energy impacts your life and ripples out into the world.

Completing this journey is an incredible feat, which I'm sure had many twists, turns, peaks, and valleys. I invite you to celebrate this accomplishment and bathe in all the good vibes. It can be human nature to skip the celebration and jump right to the next thing, but the sacred feminine luxuriates in the *pause*. So let this energy simmer, integrate, and become part of your daily life.

Oftentimes, after major shifts and stages of growth there can be a lull, low, or comedown period. A spiritual jetlag if you will. I recommend riding it out, being gentle with yourself, and trusting that this is all part of the process. Let it be part of a juicy feminine period of receiving, of resting, of celebrating.

Part of human nature is that we forget who we truly are. All of the practices in this book are built to be guideposts on your path back to yourself. Know, that anytime you are feeling removed from your Inner Goddess, you can jump right back into this work as a way of coming home to your heart. Open a "random" page for inspiration or divine guidance whenever you need.

Remember, we are all connected, and by you taking on this duty of radical wholeness, you are uplifting all of humanity. I bow to you, your bravery, your heart, and your dedication to heaven on Earth. You are Goddess embodied and I love you.

Om Shanti. Om Peace.

Author Biography

Lauren Leduc is a beloved yoga teacher and spiritual life coach. Based in Kansas City, Missouri, she is the owner of True Love Yoga Studio and founder of Pop-Up Yoga KC. She is a world traveler, yoga retreat leader, yoga teacher trainer, and new Mama. Lauren has the unique gift of cultivating community, empowering others to be their highest selves, and mentoring future feminine leaders. *Embody Your Inner Goddess: A Guided Journey to Radical Wholeness* is Lauren's first literary work.

Note to Reader

Thank you for purchasing *Embody Your Inner Goddess: A Guided Journey to Radical Wholeness*. My sincere hope is that you derived as much from reading this book as I have in creating it. If you have a few moments, please feel free to add your review of the book at your favorite online site for feedback. Also, if you would like to connect with me, other readers, my online community, retreats, and more, please visit laurenleduc.com.

Sincerely,
Lauren Leduc

O-BOOKS

SPIRITUALITY

O is a symbol of the world, of oneness and unity; this eye represents knowledge and insight. We publish titles on general spirituality and living a spiritual life. We aim to inform and help you on your own journey in this life.
If you have enjoyed this book, why not tell other readers by posting a review on your preferred book site?

Recent bestsellers from O-Books are:

Heart of Tantric Sex
Diana Richardson
Revealing Eastern secrets of deep love and intimacy to Western couples.
Paperback: 978-1-90381-637-0 ebook: 978-1-84694-637-0

Crystal Prescriptions
The A-Z guide to over 1,200 symptoms and their healing crystals
Judy Hall
The first in the popular series of eight books, this handy little guide is packed as tight as a pill-bottle with crystal remedies for ailments.
Paperback: 978-1-90504-740-6 ebook: 978-1-84694-629-5

Take Me To Truth

Undoing the Ego

Nouk Sanchez, Tomas Vieira

The best-selling step-by-step book on shedding the Ego, using the teachings of *A Course In Miracles*.

Paperback: 978-1-84694-050-7 ebook: 978-1-84694-654-7

The 7 Myths about Love...Actually!

The Journey from your HEAD to the HEART of your SOUL

Mike George

Smashes all the myths about LOVE.

Paperback: 978-1-84694-288-4 ebook: 978-1-84694-682-0

The Holy Spirit's Interpretation of the New Testament

A Course in Understanding and Acceptance

Regina Dawn Akers

Following on from the strength of *A Course In Miracles*, NTI teaches us how to experience the love and oneness of God.

Paperback: 978-1-84694-085-9 ebook: 978-1-78099-083-5

The Message of A Course In Miracles

A translation of the Text in plain language

Elizabeth A. Cronkhite

A translation of *A Course In Miracles* into plain, everyday language for anyone seeking inner peace. The companion volume, *Practicing A Course In Miracles*, offers practical lessons and mentoring.

Paperback: 978-1-84694-319-5 ebook: 978-1-84694-642-4

Your Simple Path

Find Happiness in every step

Ian Tucker

A guide to helping us reconnect with what is really important in our lives.

Paperback: 978-1-78279-349-6 ebook: 978-1-78279-348-9

365 Days of Wisdom

Daily Messages To Inspire You Through The Year

Dadi Janki

Daily messages which cool the mind, warm the heart and guide you along your journey.

Paperback: 978-1-84694-863-3 ebook: 978-1-84694-864-0

Body of Wisdom

Women's Spiritual Power and How it Serves

Hilary Hart

Bringing together the dreams and experiences of women across the world with today's most visionary spiritual teachers.

Paperback: 978-1-78099-696-7 ebook: 978-1-78099-695-0

Dying to Be Free

From Enforced Secrecy to Near Death to True Transformation

Hannah Robinson

After an unexpected accident and near-death experience, Hannah Robinson found herself radically transforming her life, while a remarkable new insight altered her relationship with her father, a practising Catholic priest.

Paperback: 978-1-78535-254-6 ebook: 978-1-78535-255-3

The Ecology of the Soul

A Manual of Peace, Power and Personal Growth for Real People in the Real World

Aidan Walker

Balance your own inner Ecology of the Soul to regain your natural state of peace, power and wellbeing.

Paperback: 978-1-78279-850-7 ebook: 978-1-78279-849-1

Not I, Not other than I

The Life and Teachings of Russel Williams

Steve Taylor, Russel Williams

The miraculous life and inspiring teachings of one of the World's greatest living Sages.

Paperback: 978-1-78279-729-6 ebook: 978-1-78279-728-9

On the Other Side of Love

A woman's unconventional journey towards wisdom

Muriel Maufroy

When life has lost all meaning, what do you do?

Paperback: 978-1-78535-281-2 ebook: 978-1-78535-282-9

Practicing A Course In Miracles

A translation of the Workbook in plain language, with mentor's notes

Elizabeth A. Cronkhite

The practical second and third volumes of The Plain-Language *A Course In Miracles*.

Paperback: 978-1-84694-403-1 ebook: 978-1-78099-072-9

Quantum Bliss

The Quantum Mechanics of Happiness, Abundance, and Health

George S. Mentz

Quantum Bliss is the breakthrough summary of success and spirituality secrets that customers have been waiting for.

Paperback: 978-1-78535-203-4 ebook: 978-1-78535-204-1

The Upside Down Mountain

Mags MacKean

A must-read for anyone weary of chasing success and happiness – one woman's inspirational journey swapping the uphill slog for the downhill slope.

Paperback: 978-1-78535-171-6 ebook: 978-1-78535-172-3

Your Personal Tuning Fork

The Endocrine System

Deborah Bates

Discover your body's health secret, the endocrine system, and 'twang' your way to sustainable health!

Paperback: 978-1-84694-503-8 ebook: 978-1-78099-697-4

Readers of ebooks can buy or view any of these bestsellers by clicking on the live link in the title. Most titles are published in paperback and as an ebook. Paperbacks are available in traditional bookshops. Both print and ebook formats are available online.

Find more titles and sign up to our readers' newsletter at http://www.johnhuntpublishing.com/mind-body-spirit

Follow us on Facebook at https://www.facebook.com/OBooks/ and Twitter at https://twitter.com/obooks